MINIMALISM

How Minimalist Living Can Help You To Declutter, Tidy Up Your Stuff and Say Goodbye to Things

(The Path to an Organized, Stress-free and Decluttered Life)

Timothy Kline

Published By

Timothy Kline

All Rights Reserved

Minimalism: How Minimalist Living Can Help You To Declutter, Tidy Up Your Stuff and Say Goodbye to Things (The Path to an Organized, Stress-free and Decluttered Life)

ISBN 978-1-77485-364-1

All rights reserved. No part of this guide may be reproduced in any form without permission in writing from the publisher except in the case of brief quotations embodied in critical articles or reviews.

Legal & Disclaimer

The information contained in this book is not designed to replace or take the place of any form of medicine or professional medical advice. The information in this book has been provided for educational and entertainment purposes only.

The information contained in this book has been compiled from sources deemed reliable, and it is accurate to the best of the Author's knowledge; however, the Author cannot guarantee its accuracy and validity and cannot be held liable for any errors or omissions. Changes are periodically made to this book. You must consult your doctor or get professional medical advice before using any of the suggested remedies, techniques, or information in this book.

Upon using the information contained in this book, you agree to hold harmless the Author from and against any damages, costs, and expenses, including any legal fees potentially resulting from the application of any of the information provided by this guide. This disclaimer applies to any damages or injury caused by the use and application, whether directly or indirectly, of any advice or information presented, whether for breach of contract, tort, negligence, personal injury, criminal intent, or under any other cause of action.

You agree to accept all risks of using the information presented inside this book. You need to consult a professional medical practitioner in order to ensure you are both able and healthy enough to participate in this program.

TABLE OF CONTENTS

INTRODUCTION 1

CHAPTER 1: WHY WE WANT THINGS WE DON'T NEED? 3

CHAPTER 2: MINIMALIST LIFESTYLE IS ABOUT FREEDOM .. 9

CHAPTER 3: HOW TO BECOME A MINIMALIST 19

CHAPTER 4: THE MYTHS ABOUT MINIMALISM 30

CHAPTER 5: REST 39

CHAPTER 6: THE LIVING ROOM 49

CHAPTER 7: MINIMALIST MINDSET FOR THE FAMILY 66

CHAPTER 8: MINIMALISM FOR YOUR WHOLE LIFE 77

CHAPTER 9: THE STORY BEGINS IN THE MIND 86

CHAPTER 10: LEARNING HOW TO TURN OFF 95

CHAPTER 11: DECLUTTERING YOUR HOME 101

CHAPTER 12: TRACKING EARNINGS AND YOUR EXPENDITURES 107

CHAPTER 13: GENERAL MINIMALIST LIVING TIPS 123

CHAPTER 14: THE BEST WAY TO SORT TRASH INTO SPECIFIC TYPES 127

CHAPTER 15: THE MINIMALIST LIFESTYLE: HOW TO LIVE A SIMPLE LIFESTYLE 131

CHAPTER 16: MAKING OVER BATHROOMS 141

CHAPTER 17: MINIMIZING YOUR RELATIONSHIPS 152

CHAPTER 18: REDEFINING YOUR LIFESTYLE 156

CHAPTER 19: WHAT TO BEGIN BY LIVING A MINIMALIST LIFESTYLE 172

CONCLUSION 182

Introduction

Do you want to lead an easier, less cluttered life? Do you want to have more time and money to pursue the activities you would like to accomplish? Would you like to have the opportunity to move more freely within your own life? If so, then minimalistism is the right choice for you. Learn the advantages, strategies that will help you overcome the feelings of reducing the items within your home, and how to carry on the process of decluttering throughout your entire life. I wrote this book after my wife and me decided to sell our house and reduce our size I was astonished by the number of my friends and family members who stated that they'd like to do the similar process. When I inquired about the reasons they didn't take the plunge and they had numerous reasons that they were unable to do. As they worked to get the courage to downsize, they weren't sure where to begin or how to deal with the emotions and feelings of sadness when we let a few of our possessions go. In this book, you'll receive advice from someone who has successfully accomplished two major downsizings in my home. This is not a guidebook written by someone who lives in the middle of a huge house, that is filled with toys of all kinds and appointing you to tackle something they've not done before. I am always looking for ways to simplify. As I've reduced my size, I've discovered myself with more time and money to pursue things that many who are burdened with all their possessions wish they could do. It's not easy for everyone However, as I have learned that it can be extremely rewarding. You will feel more confident and this will give you the strength and motivation to take on other important aspects of your daily life.

Chapter 1: Why We Want things we don't need?

Before we go too far into reducing our possessions Let's talk about why we are compelled to spend so much. What brought us to the point we are at now? Our emotions and various forces are at work against us since the modern era. Businesses realize that people purchase emotions and not just objects. For instance, Harley Davidson is not the most expensive motorcycle you could purchase at a reasonable price however, when you purchase the Harley you've invested in the ethereal, personal and how it can make you feel. Harley owners have an almost cult-like following for the brand. They wear all the Harley clothing and logo tattoos and are a part of Harley groups. If you're a owner and are upset because I didn't say it's the best bike you can purchase at a reasonable price, then you're experiencing an emotional connection to the company.

In the past when people were buying items they required. Then the Industrial Age brought about mass manufacturing of goods which were usually hand-crafted. Also, wages increased as Americans began spending more. Fast forward to the 1920's. Sigmund Freud's nephew Edward Bernays was an Austrian-American who was referred to as, "The Father of Consumerism". Bernays utilized psychoanalysis to influence people to buy items they didn't really require. In the beginning, he described his techniques as "propaganda" however, the Nazis used this term to their advantage throughout World War II, and Bernays invented"Public Relations" "Public Relations". Bernays also referred to it as "Consent Engineering". The first time he used psychoanalysis was in the world of consumer goods when a tobacco company was trying to tap into the female market to take up smoking. In the early days smoking was only for men. Bernays hired beautiful, young ladies to smoke his what he called "Torches of Liberty" during the New York Easter Parade in 1929. He then approached the press and explained to them that these women were proving that they were just like men by smoking their torch of freedom. The media took pictures and before long, newspapers across the country carried pictures of these independent, strong gorgeous women smoking. The strategy worked, and sales of cigarettes for women increased dramatically. Tobacco companies created cigarettes exclusively for women. In later times, ad campaigns such as "You've made a great stride baby" were created.

Nowadays, we are bombarded by advertisements that are designed to convince us to purchase things that we don't really require. We've all fallen for it, perhaps because we were unaware of the psychological aspect of consumerism. There is a saying that you cannot force someone to purchase something they don't need However, you can induce them to purchase something they don't want. Today, we are aware and are aware of how emotions affects our buying choices.

Sugar High

There is an emotional component to the loss or gain of possessions. We've all bought one item (or to me personally, many things) and felt the excitement when we left the shop with that unique item that we have to have. It's like an adrenaline rush. It is similar to a sugar high then use it just for a few times, and it's not utilized. Sometimes, it sits in our home for a long time without being used. The sugar rush doesn't last for long and there's a short time when people feel good. People are always drawn to satisfaction, and go to any lengths to stay away from pain. The thought of buying that particular product feels happy is a more attractive thought to some than the thought of going out without the product. Going out of the store without that item can trigger thoughts of "I would like to have it but I can't afford this" or "Everyone owns it, so why isn't me?"

Look at your home now. Do you remember purchasing the things you see? Do you remember the thing that was in the corner was cool? Do not feel guilty. Advertisers have made use of our emotions to make us purchase products and even promote for these items. Check out all the cars in the roadways with logos on the back of their cars. Is the guy ahead of you who wears an Yeti cooler sticker and a Costa sunglasses on his vehicle truly care about these items so very much? Are we really concerned whether he endorses these items? No. They might be excellent items, but there's the reason why is so passionate about these products. The man believes he's part of a group or something like, "I can afford a $2000 cooler and expensive glasses". There's a reason an individual such as Bill Gates does not have the "Yeti" label on their Bentley. Gates does not believe that it is his duty to be part of this particular group. Advertisers have targeted specifically the people in this category and have built an identity that is tied to their product.

The truth is that there's an element of emotion when we purchase items we don't actually require. Many of us believe that these products will make us feel more comfortable. You get that short feeling of happiness and often feeling part of something greater than ourselves. Sometimes, the reason could be jealousy. Some people may be compensating for something missing from our lives. It is important to recognize that there's an emotional element of buying items we don't really need. Be aware of our emotional purchasing will allow us to pause and contemplate the next purchase. Understanding the emotional connection to our possessions can also assist us in reduce their size and keep us from falling into the same situation time and time.

Chapter 2: Minimalist Lifestyle Is About Freedom

If you're not certain if minimalism is an ideal choice, take a look at how difficult it would be to relocate with lots of belongings. Moving homes and moving with lots of clutter and lots of things isn't a lot of fun, and this is when all the things isn't needed can bite you in the back.

The aim is to limit your possessions to what aren't necessary and to items that you enjoy and that are important to you. Once you've done that you will find moving simpler and more efficient. Moving is not an easy task and it's not required to make it difficult.

It will also give you the possibility of putting all of your possessions in a backpack and travelling around the globe at your own time. The world is yours when you accomplish this. It is also possible to rent your house while you travel to be truly efficient.

This is just one illustration of the way that having less clutter allows you to be more free. Being able to travel the world in this manner would not be as feasible when you have a lot of stuff to weigh you down. You can't be more flexible when you've got many things to contend with and it's in a way, similar to being stuck. I am confident that you'll feel as like a feather when you don't have a lot of mess around you, weighing your down.

Create a Space to Zen

There are many ways that being able to reduce your clutter can be a great way to relax. One additional example is the fact that having less things results in less stress. It is said that a house is a reflection of its owner's attitude. It is normal for life to be busy for any person at certain moments and homes could be a reflection of an atmosphere that feels as if all the weight of the world is the top of the person who owns it. It is easy to have clutter pile up all over the place and it could be difficult to find a way to tackling the clutter.

The sink might be overflowing with dishes or papers may be lying around , and it isn't easy to unwind in these circumstances Even when the time to relax arrives it is difficult to make maximum benefit from your time of relaxation as the chaos of the house acts as an omen of all the troubles.

If your home is messy, there's always the feeling of tasks that need to be completed. This makes it even more difficult to be relaxed and relax your mind.

Even if you're doing everything perfectly in terms of minimalism is concerned it is possible to encounter instances where things don't go as planned. is in order and this will make you feel stressed because things aren't going as you would like them to. To combat this, you need to make your space a place of Zen and that is any space or room inside your house where there is never any clutter. The style of that space will be more minimalist and this can be achieved with the help of more rules , such as drinking or eating food is not permitted inside, or being permitted to enter with shoes.

The purpose of having an area in your home that is clean and tidy regardless of what happens is to ensure that you have a space that you can to sit and be able to block out from the outside world as you engage in a relaxing or reading book.

Reduce the time you spend cleaning

As previously mentioned that you'll spend much less time cleaning after you live in a minimalist home and this can also reduce the amount of work required to ensure that things are in order since you're using effective methods.

It's a fact many people are spending more time than they prefer doing tasks that don't provide much enjoyment however they have to be done like washing the laundry , dishwashing, or ironing their clothes or other task. These chores can take up the time you could have spent in activities that you enjoy, like having time with friends that are important to you or undertaking something more important, such as writing a novel.

A great deal of the monotonous aspects of your life can be cut down by reducing your clutter or doing something so easy as having less possessions can dramatically reduce the amount of time you'd otherwise spend cleaning up. Similar principles can be applied to any other item you own and will help in reducing the time that you are occupied with chores, so that the time can be spent on something you are passionate about.

If you're planning to take this one step further it is essential to be able to establish systems that will ensure that the job is done more efficiently. As an example, investing in a dishwasher can remove the need cleaning the dishes by hand and, while the entire chore of cleaning the dishes is performed by the machine, you are able to do other things like tackling another task. Dishwashers can be costly upfront however, they can help you save time and money, and you'll recognize that a variety of decisions in life are the choice between the time and money.

You can design strategies for many other things like documents to help you arrange them in the least amount of time as you can. It is also possible to create plans for the clothes you'll wear to allow you to make fewer decisions , which can help you do not suffer from decision fatigue. There's a reason the majority of successful people utilize this hack.

There is no doubt, encountered one of these robotic vacuum cleaners. Investing in one is an excellent idea if really want to cut back on time spent cleaning.

To summarize the essence of all these examples minimalism doesn't only concern how things look, but it's as much about ensuring that a particular place needs minimum maintenance and upkeep, that nobody really wants to perform. This could even mean choosing meals that require less time to cook, even although they might not taste as great as other choices that may require more preparation time.

Achieve Financial Freedom

Perhaps the most significant aspect of being a minimalist is that you'll be able to purchase some financial freedom because you are less dependent and less things that are just necessities. That means your costs are considerably lower and the amount that you will need to be happy is significantly less. This will make life much simpler and more enjoyable as you will not worry about finances since there won't be as much debt that would make you do things you do not would like to do.

Wealth isn't just about the amount of money you make It's about the difference between what you make and the amount you spend. If you can reduce the amount you invest, your money will increase and that's what can give you choices for your future.

After having read through this article, it'll be evident to you that you don't have to pile up things in your home to feel fulfilled and to make your house an enjoyable place to be in. Although avoiding buying numerous unnecessary items is an excellent piece of advice, it's advised to get rid of items aren't used for and it can prove beneficial in terms of saving money is involved. If you're here, there's likely you're an Android user. should you be concerned about being the most current model, you could swap your current phone for the most recent model as soon as it becomes available. you'll be able to purchase the most recent model at minimum cost at the time of.

Similar to that you could also save money by making use of the things you already have and being thrifty instead of purchasing new items. To be able to do this, it is important to know in advance what you enjoy doing so that you are capable of doing whatever you wish to do. In the end, you'll be able to spend more of your energy and time on worthwhile things, such as reading books.

If there's a ways to make life simpler while maintaining the things and activities that you love, try it. If you follow the advice by this article, you'll save a lot of money in the long run and can enjoy your life without worry being able to relax knowing you don't need to be worried about paying off debt or wondering if you could be able to afford something that can bring you joy. This relaxed lifestyle will ensure that you're much happier than you could be if you owned many things.

Your entire life can be planned based on these principles and by adopting this type of mindset, you'll immediately consider purchasing smaller houses instead of a bigger one, which means your mortgage payments are lower, and you will be able to have more money to spend and more freedom.

Chapter 3: How to Become a Minimalist

Being a minimalist is a long-winded process. It's the method to get rid of clutter in your life and get it easier to keep it in order. The most important thing is that it is an ongoing process or routine. It's not possible to just sit down one day and clean up all the clutter, only to put it away. It will come back within a couple of days. It is necessary follow a method to eliminate clutter and stop it from re-entering your home.

Set Rules

If you want to become minimalist, one method isn't the best for all. You'll need to establish guidelines that are suitable for your needs. You must decide beforehand what things cause the most quantity of clutter in your home and eliminate them in a methodical manner.

Guidelines for getting rid of clutter out of your work space, home and your personal life can't be the same for all areas of your life. Every area requires a different approach. So, you'll need decide how you'd like your life to appear when you've trimmed the things you need to take care of.

The first step is mark the areas where you'll need to focus your efforts. If you're looking to eliminate the clutter from your home take note of those areas that require cleaning the most. If you're looking to tidy your office, you need to identify the clutter that is taking up the space. If it's your personal life, you need to identify the items that are choking your.

It is not possible to proceed without having a clear understanding of the mess and how you'd like to get rid of them. Minimalism is an effective strategy. It is not possible to progress by muddled thinking. It is, however, an organized method. The cleaning should begin at one location. Find the areas that require attention and work and work hard to eliminate the clutter and get free.

Stay Concentrated

It is a habit we make with the passage of time. It's not an simple task to let the desire to keep things. Every item we have in our lives has some significance. When you're cleaning, it's not uncommon to have the impression that they could be useful in the near future. This has resulted in the accumulation of clutter. You'll have to resist the urge and continue to clean.

Minimalism is about identifying items that are useful immediately and those which aren't. It is possible to further classify them into those which are utilized sporadically, as well as those which haven't been extensively used. Storing things for future use is likely to result in an increase in chaos and confusion. The ability to see the purpose of items is among the most essential elements of living an minimalist life style.

We live in a world where everything is quick and simple. If you'll require these items in the future they are available any time you'd like. They will cost you time and space.

So, when you start cleaning this basic idea should remain in your head.

If You Don't Use It, Lose It

There are many things that haven't seen daylight of day for quite some time. These items aren't likely to see a better outcome at any time in the future. But, you have these items because you don't use them or believe that you'll utilize them in the near future. Alas! The time will never come. Things would always be new and the old ones just become a burden to the storage capacity of your home.

Begin with one area and select the items that you've been using in the last few days. In addition all other items create chaos and should be removed. They are a huge burden on your soul. When you come across this subject, these thoughts are likely to keep your attention for a moment. They could trigger thoughts of regret. They will never allow you to utilize them in the first place. It are useless.

If you own clothes you've not worn in an entire season and you have purchased new clothes, then you won't be using the clothes anyway, or live without them.

If you have clothes that do not fit anymore, they're not needed anymore. If you're looking to slim down one size or smaller, you should be rewarded with more modern and superior clothes. They will always weigh in your head. This is also true for the other accessories you have that you have in your closet.

If you have equipment in your kitchen you do not use, the fact that you keep them is not doing any good. They can only make your kitchen appear messy and unorganized. This makes it difficult to work. Eliminate the items that you do not use or have a substitute for them. Don't keep them for rainy days since you'll discover a way to get there when that day does come, even without these things.

The rules of engagement are straightforward If you've not utilized the item within the last six months or in the previous season, chances are you won't make use of them again and you are able to trust that.

Organise

The main goal of minimalist living is making important items easily accessible. If you don't have a proper arrangement there is a chance that you will not have the ability to find items even if you own just a handful. It is crucial to establish an appropriate place to keep important items in your home. It is important to establish a routine to store these things in the same location. This will make retrieving them easy.

The fact that you have more essential items could cause problems at this phase. It's not just about keeping the most important items but also making most efficient use of available resources. The excess of things is likely to make you feel uncaring about them.

Reduce the amount of stuff you own and set the right place to keep them to ensure that you are able to locate them at any time you need.

Minimalism is a way of making the most of all the things you own. At first it might be hard to let go of things. But, it's an immense relief to have the most important items in their location whenever you require them. This is only possible once you give the proper importance to them and it's not going to be easy to achieve if you own lots of them.

Be tough on things That aren't in Use

There are many items in homes that are both physical as well as emotional appeal. You shouldn't just throw away anything that is emotionally appealing. But, consider asking yourself the difficult question of how often you are revisiting them. If you've been looking at them again, store them in a prominent location. Otherwise, they're of little value compared to other clutter that is occupying your home. Items that have emotional appeal are crucial but you have to make sure that they've not lost their ability to hold you.

If they are your most most treasured, then you should give an a special place for them or get rid of them. If you have several copies of something Choose the ones you wish to keep and dispose of the rest. Items that are emotionally burdensome and do not bring happiness or joy to your life must be removed. They only keep your mind cluttered and makes recovery from past traumas difficult.

Create more empty space

Making more space within your home or your life is in your own choice. You have to decide what you would like to keep as well as those that you can afford to part with. The final decision is yours. But, the level of satisfaction that empty space provides is difficult to describe in words. Space that is empty means more chances to be able to accept. It's refreshing to not carry the burden of unnecessary items. This means less work and cleaning. It's a lot less stressing about things you didn't really care for in the real world. It's a feeling of freedom.

Minimalism doesn't just mean creating space within your home, but also in your daily life. It is an extremely beneficial space because it helps you be more open. There's less to do and therefore you'll enjoy your life significantly more. When you are able to accommodate other aspects of your life, you don't have to fret about the replacement of others. This is because you're walking without moral burdens from the past, or painting on a clean white wall.

Be selective about the items You Take

A minimalist lifestyle and staying free of clutter is a way of life. It requires patience and you must be conscious of the work. Before you bring something new into your home or into your life, you'll need to think about the significance of the item and what value it brings in your daily life. If it adds worth to you and provides something that you are happy that other items already in your life were not capable of and bring joy to you, then you must bring it in. If you don't choose carefully when you add something, you'll end up with more than you were able to eliminate initially.

In the process of adding new items should be gradual and careful. If you're adding something, consider what you can eliminate to ensure there's no additional clutter. Stress your importance to the new item and the positive changes it can bring to your daily life. Think about whether the item can be utilized regularly or not.

A minimalist lifestyle is a conscious choice. This method keeps you in order and free. It requires an organized approach to the process of selection.

The minimalistic approach to life can have many benefits. It keeps your clutter at bay and well-organized. It allows you to use objects to their maximum potential because you only have items you will need. It helps you save cash as you purchase less and concentrate on maximizing the value of your investment.

Chapter 4: The Myths about Minimalism

Minimalism can be boring.

A minimalist lifestyle isn't free of enjoyment or pleasure. It is a way to eliminate some of the everyday chores (organizing shopping, organizing and cleaning) that take away the joy of a day. Once useless items are gone minimalism allows the minimalist to choose what is important to them in their lives. Many will decide to travel around the globe, do impossible tasks, stay at home, or mix up their family living lives.

Minimalists do not own high-end items.

One of the wonderful undiscovered benefits of in a minimalist lifestyle is the opportunity to buy things of higher quality. Because of various reasons, people aren't able to connect owning less items with proudly possessing more expensive items. In reality, they are simultaneously connected. When we make a decision to purchase fewer items that we can live with, we are exposed for the prospect of having more expensive items as well.

Minimalism is devoid and empty.

One of the first things we did following our transition to minimalistism is to look over our home and eliminate every ornament that wasn't huge or stunning, but we didn't take them all off. The final ornament in our home, we were able to determine its importance to us and as a result visitors are able to discern what is most important to us. Our walls aren't empty. They are filled with lifestyles. We strive for rational minimalism, but not extreme minimalistism. However, for more details about how minimalists can beautify their homes, check out adding warmth without adding things by Francine Jay.

Minimalists are a bit snobby .

I'm the first to admit that a small percentage of humans make use of minimalism as a way to lead a lazy selfish, ineffective life. But this doesn't represent the majority of minimalists I have come to realize. The majority of minimalists I know carry the same burdens (art work, circle of relatives, the society) in the same way as those who aren't. Although a small percentage have adopted minimalistism as a means to leave their job or as means to pursue their artistic pursuits they are passionate about. It's probably an extremely high-quality item.

Minimalists are ardent environmentalists.

Minimalism is a good thing for the environmental. People who adhere to minimalism eat less and dispose of less waste, and this is a blessing for everyone. However, not everyone who is a minimalist is doing so because of environmental motives. Personally, my pursuit to be minimalist is an expression of discontent over the direction my life is taking. I became annoyed by the amount of time, money, and energy that ended up getting oriented towards the things in my life instead of the relationships. As I embraced minimalist living, I decided to have more chances to live in my highest beliefs... in addition to help to improve the health of the world as I went along.

Minimalists are vegetarians or vegans.

It is my personal choice to be a minimalist. I eat meat and vegetables as do countless minimalists are like me.

Minimalism means giving up everything belongings to you

Strangely to me, certain people seem to believe that minimising means throwing out all of it or, at the very least almost the entire amount. This isn't the case whatsoever. Instead, minimalism is about living with less and, as I often affirm, less isn't the same as no. If you walk into my home in the present, you'll likely not be expecting the family is minimalist. In our living space there's seats for four people, a circle of photos of our relatives and a rug, as well as an espresso desk, as well as our most basic television. Inside our closet for coats, you will discover baseball caps, jackets as well as winter-climate-related accessories. In the rooms of our kids you'll find books, craft materials and toys within the closets. We want to live a simple life but at the same moment, we're living, breathing, changing humans. To live is to eat. We still own things. However, we've worked hard to rid ourselves of the excessive collection of things. I frequently talk about "rational minimalistism" as well as "strategic minimalistism" to understand what I'm talking about. I'm not suggesting eliminating everything that is humanly feasible. Instead, I urge people to eliminate everything that isn't necessary so that they may achieve their goals in life. I am passionate about my heart as well as my family and about influencing and loving other people. I am aware of these values above all else.

Minimalism can be a means to these ends for me.

It eliminates physical distractions to help me focus on my main priorities. This is why I completely eliminate the things I must be in line with my goals. However, if I find things that allow me to live my life as I'd like I keep them and enjoy these things. I'm not ashamed of these things at all. It might be the same to you if you decide to walk through the

Minimalism is about organizing Your possessions

The art of organizing has its place. However, it's not the same as minimising. Take a look. Organising our belongings (without eliminating the clutter) is the most effective short-term solution. It is a process that should be repeated and over. My friend and fellow minimalist Courtney Carver places it, "If you could organize your stuff would you not be able to do it in the near future?" At its heart organizing is essentially changing the order of things. Although we might discover storage solutions today however, we could be forced to search for new ones by tomorrow. Also, organizing our belongings (without put off) isn't without flaws:

It's not beneficial to everyone other than you.

Things we rarely utilize are stored in cabinets in our attics, basements and garages. They provide little benefit at all same time as the people around us could benefit from these cabinets.

Organizing doesn't resolve our debt problems.

This does not solve the root issue of why we purchase too many things. Sometimes moving our belongings frees us more when we buy containers, garage units or bigger homes to house it.

Organizing doesn't turn back our desire for extra.

The process of arranging our belongings into bins, plastic containers or even extra closets is about holding on to our accumulation of excess. In this way, it always impedes our desire to seek satisfaction with our stuff.

The process of organizing doesn't require us to look at our lives.

While organizing our possessions might cause us to look at every item we have but it doesn't require us to consider whether we would like to keep them. We often put them in containers and put them near the lids and then forget about them we do.

The process of organizing is not very effective in setting the stage for future adjustments.

Organising may also give temporary lift to our moods because it results in a tidyer home but it never amounts to a real exchange in lifestyle. Our minds are that our house is too small, our money isn't enough and we can't find enough time in the daytime. There is also the possibility of rearranging our belongings, but not our lives. However, the act of removing possessions in our homes fulfills several of these goals. It transforms our hearts and alters our lives. It's also an eternal solution, not more a temporary one that we'll need to be able to repeat. When we've eliminated the item, it's gone for good. The process of organizing is more effective than anything else. However, minimizing is more important so the.

Chapter 5: Rest

I know I'm sure. If another person advises you to take a break and not worry so much then you're bound to hit them with a slap. That's why I am so happy to speak to you from an author's pages and not face-to-face. (Did that sentence made you laugh? It's okay, check out the previous chapters).

Sleepcations, Staycations, and Other ways to relax

The process of complete relaxing, complete and rejuvenating is not easy to attain. But regardless of the degree of stress that is affecting your life currently You can get rid of the stress and tension by going on a trip!

I know, I'm aware. It's likely that you don't have the time or resources to go to the Bahamas or even Boston for an enjoyable, luxurious getaway. That's fine.

Do you have two hours?

This means that even if you're currently living without income and have little time to spare it is possible to enjoy some time away from the pressures of daily life. This is the nature of living a minimalist lifestyle that requires only a few hours and a tiny (or in certain cases, not much) cash, you can enjoy huge benefits.

Go back to the natural world. If you are immersed in your natural surroundings and get in touch with nature, you can clean your mind and cleanse your soul. You'll relax and recharge by interacting with nature's that has a bounty of the flora and fauna that delights the senses.

Your very own nature-inspired paradise can take the form of your own backyard and, if not garden at present it is possible to get started! Enjoy the heavenly beautiful, ethereal splendor of pink roses, or the ethereal scent of lavender Lilacs, or maybe some Emerald Ferns.

Maybe the beach is than you're looking for. Enjoy a dip in the water of cool azure or build castles out of gold sand. Engage in a vigorous beach volleyball game, or stroll along the shoreline.

Explore the world of art. In addition to being a creative outlet and expression art will allow you to escape the world for a brief period.

If you can write a wacky tale of fantasy or create an imaginative scene you imagine in your head and you want to go to a different, more beautiful world that is your own design, in which there is nothing that is out of your control. It is possible to express your thoughts and feelings in a secure and productive way while releasing tension while you immerse yourself in the making of something wonderful.

Go on an excursion for a day. If you've got a day off, do not stay in your bedroom, stressing and worrying about your worries. Instead, go to a relaxing and relaxing spot where you can unwind and play with your kids again, with minimal harm to your wallet. Go to a movie. Go to an art gallery or an aquarium, an herb garden or planetarium, or a museum, or the restaurant. Enjoy an athletic event. Have a picnic or a stroll through the park. Enjoy the music at a live performance, or go to a karaoke club where you can sing your favourite tunes. Find out more about your most-loved topics at your local library or at the bookstore, Both should provide comfortable chairs and tables to make your life easier. Explore the world in a shopping mall you love. Also, do things you enjoy just for the sake of it, and for your mental well-being!

Eat and rest.

"Wow this is amazing tips!" You might be thinking now. "You are telling me to complete two essential things that I need to complete everyday just to make it through the day! Thanks much, Einstein!"

It is now clear that you take in food and rest regularly and on a nightly basis. But if you're distressed and stressed, you might not be sleeping or eating in the amount you need to and, in contrast it could be that you are doing too much of either or both.

When you are engaged in both activities, relax and relax. Consume delicious and nutritious meals that are based on vegetables and fruits juices, teas and juices.

You might be looking at your feet at this suggestion, or you can hear your mother's voice within your mind, urging you to eat your vegetables! But it's true when you eat well and are active, your energy will rise and your stamina will increase making you more prepared to face and conquer the difficulties and challenges that you face in your daily life. Also, believe that or not fruit and vegetables can be delicious but they aren't!

I'm not suggesting you should spend all your time eating Brussel sprouts with a side of dry carrots and a bottle of water drink (Everybody together now: Yum!). Enjoy your palate instead with smooth smoothies and fruit desserts with crisp green salads, decorated with tomatoes that are ripe with a plethora of herbs and delicious sauces. Filling, and strengthening vegetables in casseroles and lasagnas; flavorful waters and delicious fruit juices as well as sweet yogurts mixed with a variety of fruits.

Make it a habit to eat slowly, and slowly whenever possible, and to eat in the presence of your family or friends as you enjoy a conversation over all the good food. Even frozen pizza can be like a meal when shared with good-hearted, kind people.

Once you have your menu and guest list ready It is also possible to prepare the table to eat. Place your table on mats and plates and polish your silverware and invite guests into the kitchen to assist in preparing the meal. It's a way to transform an ordinary, boring job into a gathering for friends.

After you've had an energizing, delicious and satisfying meal, you will be ready to relax for the evening as opposed to shifting and turning through another tense, anxious night, you can turn your sleeping period into a restful sleep!

Have a relaxing and luxurious journey that prepares you to take on and overcome the various challenges of your life. Sleep is supposed to last a long time, be deep, and complete, removing you from the tangle of your tense existence to the tranquility of a peaceful rejuvenating, energizing, and reviving sleeping.

However, for the depressed and anxiety-ridden person experiencing a peaceful and meaningful sleep may be expensive. This is the reason it might be the perfect time to take a sleeping in!

As you settle down for your evening sleep, you might be overwhelmed by the stress of the day, your body tightening and your brain racing as you try to put aside all worries and anxieties and get a good night of sleep.

In order to make the experience more pleasant What you might require is to make sure that you have the proper setting for your sleeping.

At least an hour before the time to go to bed, switch off your mobile phone and your computer at work; lock your home office , and set aside your work time for the day.

If you enjoy watching the TV or DVD, make sure the content is soothing and not arousing; and if you decide to read, choose an enjoyable book and easy to read and also one that is relaxing and gentle on the body. If you open your briefcase to remove a report or a brief to read, you should be prepared for me to go to your home and take it out of your hands! It's not that bad, but it is important to know that mixing business and leisure is not a wise choice.

Relax in a warm bath, if you're feeling pampered and then change your work clothes to comfy pajamas. Switch off your lights, and go to your bed or, as you'll probably imagine this is the location of your nighttime escape (Can you tell that I simply love the word"sleepcation"?).

Listen to some soothing, soft music on your CD or computer No matter if these songs come from the classical, smooth jazz soft rock, the new age genre it is likely to be successful at relaxing the body as well as clearing your thoughts. Set off some candles or gently lit lamps. Drink a cup of tea or water or coffee, and read a few pages of a great book (just ensure that the book isn't too great, otherwise you'll be enticed to stay up all night and read the book!) Or, look at the picture of a soothing item in your home. It could be the aquarium of your choice, or a work of art, a photograph of a beloved one or a favorite photo.

Then, relax in a comfy bed and warm with cozy pillows and crisp, clean sheets, or maybe an inviting blanket that brings back memories of the 'blankey' you grew up with'. Do not stress about sleeping promptly so that you can get enough time to rest and prepare for the next day. It's a bit ironic, but it can only create anxiety. Instead, relax, relax, and get away. Sweet dreams!

Chapter 6: The Living Room

Although the living room is considered to be one of the rooms that is most difficult in the home to maintain a tidy appearance however, it is actually one of the easiest rooms to get rid of clutter since living rooms typically don't have many storage options, so they aren't able to hide anything.

The secret to having an orderly living space is:

* Always having storage spaces for the items you regularly need, such as books, magazines or remote controls.

* Cleaning the space often.

How do you go about it

Make sure you have four containers to organize all the things you need to sort.

Begin by removing the bookcases, consoles and side tables then move into the entertainment area as well as the coffee table. Clean these areas, and look over the things they may be storing, and then return them to their storage spaces. Place the books in the bins Return those remotes back to their appropriate locations, check your mail fold your blankets, and continue.

Moving on to the electronic devices. Begin by taking everything that isn't connected to your audio system or TV and then dispose of them in the 'trash donation/sale, recycle or put away container. Everything else that's not working, even though it's connected to these electronic devices goes into the trash container. Make sure to put all gaming devices, chargers, and other equipment in the place they're supposed to be (via the "put away" bin).

Then, you can sort the toys and evaluate the condition of each toy, assessing the wear and tear. Consider whether the toy is still working and if you children still play with it. You can either recycle or store it based on the answer you get.

How can you enhance the decor of your living space

Add a neutral color

If you are able, consider applying neutral hues to your ceiling, walls flooring, furniture and floors. The neutral palette or colors generally provide a tranquil atmosphere and also provide immediate sophistication.

Make use of small-scale furniture

If you're looking to bring an elegant, minimalist look to your living space You can do that by choosing furniture that doesn't dominate or overwhelm the room. Choose a sofa with a the back of the sofa that is upholstered tightly with thin arms, instead of one with massive arms and an upholstered back with multiple cushions.

If your living space isn't huge and you're looking for four beautiful chairs, the option of a coffee table or good loveseat are more suitable than a couch. Make sure to choose chair without arms when you are choosing chairs because they don't require up much space (or appear to be) in contrast to chairs that come with arms.

Install a chic carpet in the center of the space

It is possible to get a basic but elegant carpet, which is perfect for our needs. Make sure it is in the middle for a gorgeous space that looks quite striking and cool.

Increase the focal point

If your living space is confined to one main focal point, which is the fireplace, it is possible to enhance it in a variety of ways (depending on the type of fireplace). If there is a fireplace for instance, you could increase the size of it by having a complete focus wall. The focal wall isn't necessarily flashy, but it does be a major influence on the overall feeling and appearance of your living space. Metal panels can be used to give it a more textured look.

Utilize natural accents

There are many natural elements that can be added to your minimalist living space. Plants and natural wood as pieces of furniture, accent tables, and other items to keep the appearance easy and neutral. If you'd like to go with the plant-based approach go for a potted, good quality hanging plants and trees for your space to provide a the natural, peaceful atmosphere.

The Office
The office is most likely the most important place in your home. It could be a gorgeous well-organized space that makes work enjoyable, or a dark space that frustrates every time you walk into. Whatever the case, how you are feeling

about your work space is more influential on your productivity than you imagine!
There are a few steps it is possible to do arrange your office space in a way that is efficient and specifically the drawers that are most often the worst. This is howto:
What is really needed sitting on the desk?
The first thing to decide is what you want to put at your desk before you even open a drawer on your desk.

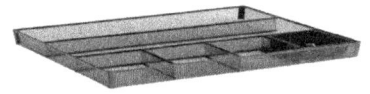

Ask yourself what you need to have the front of you every day. It could include a computer, printer as well as a teacup and glasses of water. It is also possible to have some inspirational things that aren't in the corner that will make you smile , and perhaps some markers, pens and scissors neatly kept in a glass. they can be easily accessed and then put away. If you're among people who enjoy planning and organising, you can keep your daily list of tasks at your desk.

Naturally, you may find that you need less than the amount you need. If you have more than that it is possible to rethink your office needs and, in the process dispose of, recycle recycling, move some of it into the "donate or sell" container.

Make an inventory

After you've identified what you want to put at your table, the second step you'll need to do is look through your drawers. If you're like the majority of people, then you'll discover that you've lost the majority of things within your drawers. This step is easy, simply pull them out and organize everything in your drawers into the standard four categories.

Don't rush. Take your time, and remember that removing and storing items efficiently requires a lot of time. When you're done you'll be left with the items that you need and often use.

Take the containers with the items you've put away (in this instance, these items were not in the right drawers) and recycle (which likely you swept or altered in any way) and are now ready to be taken to their appropriate homes nearer.

Note In the case of cleaning out the office The 'put away container is able to hold things that are stored in the wrong drawer as well as items which are not appropriate for the office. To make it easier you can use two containers - one labeled 'putawaydrawers' and the other the other one labelled 'put away' (which is our standard "put away" container).

Then, move on for the following step

The drawers should be organized according to the things you most frequently use to those that you are not using as much.

In the drawer that is located that is on the opposite side of your dominant hand, place things you use in the most frequent order. For example, in your left-hand top drawer (assuming you're left-handed) it is possible to have things like staplers, tape, paperclipsand post-its and rubber bands. There is also an organizer for your drawer that is shallow inside the drawer of your desk. This is ideal for keeping paper clips and pushpins away from getting mixed with rubber band.

Where can you locate drawer organizers? They are readily available in most retail stores for office supplies or on the internet at companies such as Amazon and Target. However, it's important be aware that when purchasing your organizer, you'll need to make sure the length and depth are compatible with the drawer. It is also important to find an organizer that is sturdy enough to hold all your belongings and also let you close and open the drawers with ease, without office equipment getting stuck to your table's edge.

Make a drawer for large objects

It is also important to have a second drawer that can keep some of the bulky objects that you could put on your desk and easily be put away. The desk's top drawer for that, because it is a storage space for empty file folders as well as extra printer paper. It is also possible to use the drawer to hold the purpose of a Skype headset as well as an label maker, or something similar.

Make sure you have a drawer with a file folder If you have space

If you have a drawer that is large and wide enough to accommodate files, you could utilize it for this vital task. Nowadays, all of the essential documents we've got can be stored via the cloud or an external hard drive, however there are still many benefits of keeping your working documents on paper, but , of course, in a neat and tidy place on your desk. One reason is that it ensures they are readily available to be able to access them swiftly when you need to hurry to attend an appointment, take an unplanned call, or tackle a major task.

However, the most important thing to do in maintaining your office clean in this case is to develop a habit of recycling or shredding documents at the point they are no longer relevant. To keep your office

clutter-free make sure the drawer you have that is designated for the folders and files you have is a living organism that is not just a fossil-bed for all the work that you've completed in the last fifteen years.
Sort the drawers according to their function

Now you must arrange your other drawers according to the way they can help you. I personally like to have a drawer for money as well as one for mail things. The mail drawer may be filled with things like thank-you cards or blank cards, return-address labels, cards for special occasions, envelopes and stamps.
In the drawer of finances You can find checkbooks, a fire-safe container with passports, and all of the essential documents. If there is a particular work

you frequently do in your workplace that you believe needs specific supplies, you can try putting the items in one drawer, so that you just need to open one drawer in order to access the specific items for your task all at all times.

Keep in mind that your workstation, whether indoors or outside, should be a source of encouragement and help you stay productive Not slow you down.

At the end of the day you'll end up with things that don't have homes (in the trash and others in the 'put away basket to store things that are not needed at the workplace). You must decide the reason for these items, and ensure not to keep duplicates within the office. This means that when you have items that you don't think you can give away, take them to the closest recycling center. These three suggestions will assist you in achieving success cleaning out your office space even after you're done

Always make sure you are digital whenever possible. This means that items like business cards ought to be kept in a small amount in your office (as you can load all important contacts to computers).

The freebies you get during seminars or at conventions can never be compared to certificates of achievement or awards. They can be replaced with awards.

Think about using all-in-one devices like post-it holders and scanner printer-fax machines to reduce space.

How can you enhance your office's décor Select good textures and colors

The mood of different colors is affected in different ways. If you'd like to create a peaceful and relaxed office, go for neutral or accent colors such as grey or beige. Be aware that the color and texture are not limited to walls, but also to cushion cushions (if there is a sofa) as well as storage, pens and cushions and other small objects also.

Include the wall color in these pieces to create some interest and a few elements to your interior. Remember that minimalism doesn't need to be boring. You can experiment with textures to enhance the areas of your office.

Take down your ornaments and invest in low-maintenance plants

You've already heard that it's beneficial to have neutrality in your scheme of colors. But, if you're looking to boost your productivity, you should consider adding a some natural elements. Plants are a classic option that can be easily maintained within your workplace, like these:

Great art on the wall at eye level

Do not be afraid from putting in two or three pieces of artwork at work to promote minimalist design. A great piece of art will boost your creativity and inspire you. It can also make you more productive and happier. If you have a quality artwork, place it in a location that is convenient and easy for your eyes.

You can also add some wood furniture Materials such as wood as well as similar materials are generally associated with a warm and cozy feel. Anything that creates an inviting, warm feeling to your workplace is ideal as offices that are clean and uncluttered are often an unattractive and cold environment. Furthermore wood is an excellent option to blend nature into the office and blends well with plants.

Chapter 7: Minimalist Mindset For The Family

The concept of minimalism might sound appealing to you, but getting everyone in your family to accept and endorse the same might not be an easy task. It's a major change, and in order to implement it every family member must be aware of the concept.

It is impossible to accept minimalism until everyone understands the fundamental concepts behind minimalism. A few people have formed an idea that minimalism is merely about removing clutter away from your home. This isn't the case. Minimalism goes beyond the idea of minimalism. It's a concept that allows you to experience the world and its joy in close proximity.

The concept of minimalism can assist you in creating closer and more connected to your family. Your children will understand the importance of moral principles in their lives and the older members can become more sensitive. It provides you with the chance to reconnect with your entire family again.

But the process of getting your family members ready for the process of letting go of their possessions isn't easy so you need to be patient and cautiously. It is crucial to recognize that while you may have gotten the benefits of minimalism your family members are far from achieving this goal.

Many people like the idea of collecting items. Kids love having a lot of stuff in their rooms. They might not be using the items or playing around with them but might be unable to let them go. It's up to you to explain the advantages of minimalism.

Teenagers love their clothes. There could be hundreds of things in their wardrobe, but they aren't able to resist the desire to buy more. For them, fashion is changing more quickly than the weather and they need to have items that are trending.

However, they won't be the most quick to let go of items they don't need in the present. They are hoarders who must be controlled and making them purge will require lots of care.

It's possible to talk to your partner, but it's not going to be an easy task. If you're a mature adult you are able to reason and follow the path of logic. But, you'll require patience and considerate when you approach things.

The best method to accomplish this is to take an easy step-by-step method. Don't ask all your relatives to follow something that you cannot do it by yourself. It is also important to allow every member of your family to get familiar with the process and then follow it at their own pace. While you are following this relaxed approach, you must make sure that your family members continue making an effort.

A few ways in that you can encourage those in your home to embrace the minimalist approach are:

Make Yourself an Example

The path to charity begins at the home. If you would like the members of your household, particularly your children, to follow in your path and follow in your footsteps, then you have to walk along the path first. In the beginning, you should begin practicing minimalism on your own. Allow your family members to experience the transformation that occurs within your own life. If your family members start realizing that having less things aren't creating any more difficult, and in fact it's creating an improvement that they can begin exploring the concept.

Learn to be an attentive listener

One of the major obstacles in building a more cohesive family unit is the fact that we don't put enough importance to how to listen. This is the to the majority of discord and rebellion. If you wish to persuade the members of your household to follow the minimalism lifestyle, you must motivate them to do so. The rules you enforce won't bring you any where. Be attentive to what the family members are saying. Learn to understand their fears, concerns or limitations and only you can begin to respond appropriately.

It is essential to show that minimalism is beyond limit the amount of stuff you have. It also implies reducing clutter and organizing your belongings around you. Inform your family about the sense of liberation you will feel when you have less clutter. Help them appreciate the benefits of having less possessions and the amount of obligations associated with belongings.

Take a One-on-One Approach

Make sure you understand the specific requirements of your family members and establish specific rules for each family member at the beginning. This can help you tone down the pressure placed on a particular person. The term "minimalism" doesn't necessarily mean the same thing to everyone and doesn't need to be. Certain people may be minimalist to the point of minimalism, where they like to reduce their possessions to the bare essentials of items. While others prefer to limit things to relaxing surroundings. Minimalism encompasses more than just getting rid of things. It is about simplifying your living and putting things back organized. It is important to observe the boundaries that everyone would like to establish for him or her.

There is the possibility of establishing the rules of common areas within the house and also individual simple guidelines for your personal spaces. This will assist you to have an understanding that is more palatable of the concept of minimalism.

Explain in the way they Are Trying to be able to comprehend

The reason for a minimalist lifestyle will differ for each person within your family. It is important to know what drives the passion of every family member.

Beauty Lover

Certain people just enjoy having things properly organized and organized. A minimalist home is ideal for them since everything would be put placed in the right location. It also means placing things in their proper spot, and should any family members like the idea that's an excellent place to start.

Travel Enthusiasts

The art of living with less items can be a great source of inspiration for those who love traveling since it helps to travel lighter. They'd like to know how to live a minimalist lifestyle. The pleasure and comfort of living a life with less be very attractive to them.

The Heartfelt

Everyone has the desire to assist others. Your family member who is driven by this desire in their heart will appreciate the fact that lots of things are available for other people if he/she is able to live with only some. This could be a major reason to choose to be minimalist.

The Earth Lovers

Every one of us is creating an enormous carbon footprint on the earth through our consumption of ever more resources. Everything we create requires a certain amount of resources. It is also possible to use this argument to bring your idea into the forefront.

From encouraging kids to have less but more valuable things, to providing them with appropriate rewards through excursions and outings there are many methods to aid your family to experiment with this idea.

It is important to allow them to feel the pleasure of being able to have less and allow them to decide whether are ready to go for it.

This is pretty straightforward for the adults since they understand the reasoning of the concept. However, it is different for children as they may not be in a position of reason. It is possible to include them in the process by giving them more rewarding opportunities to participate in decluttering or organize things.

Spend more time with them and give them more attention and it could help them realize the benefits of minimalism. Kids are keenly awaiting your attention throughout their growing years.

Your goal should be making them feel something rather than letting them rely on the material world. Your kids should be encouraged to be active more often instead of playing games on the internet or watch television. Social interactions in real life ought to be higher than their time on social media sites that are digital. When children begin to live life in actual ways, it'll be more easy for them to search for experiences rather than material ones.

Create a clutter-free home

A clean and tidy home is crucial if you are trying to encourage your family members to stick to the principles of minimalism. The less they see on their property more likely they'll be inclined to accumulate clutter in their own homes. Cleaning up after themselves is a routine that people take time to pick up from their surroundings.

Set a standard for everyone to keep the place in order. Everything must be in a designated space. Many people feel that the smaller the number of stuff in the house and the more easy it is to organize things. This is a good way to begin minimalism. It is a common belief that having less stuff can be more beneficial than having to organize them.

The satisfaction of having less is a taste that has been developed. We've developed the habit of buying things over a lengthy period of time , and it's not an easy habit to break. However, once you begin taking pleasure in being less affluent and having more fun new opportunities, they will open to you, and it gets easy to let go of the lure of having things.

Making this mindset a reality at the beginning is something that could seem like a daunting task at first, but it's the only obstacle that you'll encounter. When your family members are fully on board, the road to minimalism will be the most simple path you've ever taken in all of your life.

Chapter 8: Minimalism For Your Whole Life

The examples and the arguments discussed within this publication, naturally don't just apply to your wardrobe. Items that last longer, and even a bit more costly, are great for your pocket as well as your environment the majority often.

Do you have that urge to buy a new cell phone each year? Yeah. Do you really need that newly launched phone in your pocket? Isn't it more sensible to invest in a device that's good enough to last at minimum two years? Compare, research, and calculate.

The same is true for the other electronics that surround us. The TV you've always wanted so badly, the recently launched tablet, the super-powerful sound system which makes us want to drool at the displays in the stores (even when you're living in an apartment) and you aren't capable of using the full power provided by the gadget)...

It's not just limited to electronics,, this is a principle that applies to every home. It is applicable to every room of your home. Furniture, accessories, your kitchen equipment Everything.

If you are considering buying anything, think about the following: For all items that you might be thinking about buying, take a look at ...:

Do I really need it?

Can I ever use it?

Do I get the best way to spend my money?

What is the longest time I can be sure of this product? If I spend a bit more, can I get the same item, but with a better and more durable product?

What can I do if you don't like it Do I really want it

How to carry less

Do you have each day in your purse, pockets or your backpack?

It's not something we consider often - after all, it's easy to pack everything that we believe we require in a backpack, but every item ends up becoming an additional weight. It may not be a physical weight however, it is a greater burden.

Being aware of and making sure we take care of everything we carry is a cause for concern in addition, when we think about the physical weight If you are carrying more than you need, it could cause back pain...

Just carrying around the things you require - not less, no more can be a form to reduce your clutter. It's an approach to getting lighter, having fewer concerns, and what's more, you'll have more security.

How do you find what's inside your pocket, briefcase, bag, purse in the present moment?

Take a moment to think about the objects you hold right now.

Some common exemples:

A wallet with money and all your loyalty cards, bills, photos, and cards?

Your purse, containing many items like notepads, pens (plural) and wallets and makeup kit, necessaire, tissues?

Backpack with notebook, laptop and documents, as well as pencils (plural)?

Your mobile phone has many accessories, charging cables, headphones, cables, Bluetooth phones, extra battery?

Are you sure?

Is it your watch?

Snacks?

Books?

Drug store in a portable location (we always have adhesive bandages and painkillers in case of those times of need, don't you think?)?

Which of these things do you really require?

Try it. Be aware of everything you carry. Did you make use of all of them in the past? Will you be using them in the near future? If you've used or are planning to make use of it, then that's great. If not, take into consideration the possibility that these objects are at your home or work place and only bring them whenever you absolutely need to.

For instance, your wallet

What number of documents do you carry around? Do you really require all of them at all times?

What number of credit and debit cards are you carrying in your wallet right now? If you're planning to travel from work to home, and then on to the gym or to happy hour, and then return to your home Do you really need each one? Do you really need more than one to suffice for the daily routine, even if you don't plan on to the mall?

What other documents do you have within your pocket? Do you have the 3x4 pictures that are always on hand? The loyalty card you get from the coffee shop across town you only visit there once every few months?

Consider that, in addition to having less to worry about in your bag and having a lighter weight, carrying less items also makes it less stressful in the event that - hopefully! You happen to lose your wallet in some way. If you don't have all of your important data all the time, you have significantly fewer cards that you can remove and fewer documents that need to request.

Take a look at every item you carry every day and see if any of them can be left at home, and only take them off when absolutely necessary.

It's quite enjoyable to be able to walk around with less weight. It makes you feel more relaxed and less stressed with fewer distractions. You can also concentrate on the things that matter more to you instead of worrying about missing one of the 100 items that you carry around every day.

Your day-to-day minimalism

The principles of minimalism we discussed in this book aren't only to analyze your purse or backpack. it's an expression of your day-to-day life.

It's the desk at your office;

It's applicable to the items within your living room.

It's the same for kitchen cabinets.

It's also true for drawers

It is, of course, for your clothes as you can see here.

Keep in mind one of the two key principles of minimalism: only having the things you require, not more or less.

Do you have the desk that has the things you require? Are you sure? The pen holder that is in the middle of your desk, with six pens that a few businesses provided with their logos and two mechanical pencils that don't have graphite, a pencil you do not use, and a plethora of clippings for paper in the bottom of the holder, so that when you're in need of them, you'll have to remove everything and create a huge mess?

What about that wall decoration you put up a few years ago, which has now been transformed into a landscape in your living room that isn't making sense or coordinating with anything like the gold Eiffel Tower an ex-colleague gave you when he was in France and it doesn't make sense to you because it's not in your style You don't talk to this person anymore , and you haven't been to Paris by yourself?

Then, it is crystal obvious: if you do not take a moment to think about what do, we'll find ourselves with excess everywhere. Excessiveness only means an increase in cost along with more mess and time spent dealing with them.

Make changes to your routine and reduce time, money and keep your home clutter-free.

The most difficult thing to do is not always to clean the home and get rid of clutter. It is about becoming aware and committing to it. It's realizing that what you've got rid of is not actually necessary. Therefore, you don't need to purchase anything new. It's not necessary to buy in a hurry.

It's generally necessary to keep in mind every day when you keep things to an absolute minimum and are organized it makes life simpler. There's less time spent fixing cleaning, less time to wash and less items to careof, and it's more time-efficient to exercise and do things that are that is healthy for you.

And it is essential to recognize that minimalism doesn't have to be expressed only in objects of material and how the house , it organizes everything. Be aware that minimalism can be evident in your work and relationships as well as your way of thinking and living. Be aware that you don't need to accomplish or do too many things. You also , you don't need to accomplish too little. It's about doing and having what's essential.

Chapter 9: The Story Begins in the Mind

Within the brain, you will find many regions that are able to handle logic and deal with memories and emotions. The subconscious mind combines the events of your life and recollects the events you believe are important. It keeps track of habits and recalls reactions because it is able to start to take over faster than your conscious mind. If you visit the store to purchase something and you don't have to think about what you're doing as all the emotions of joy and happiness that you experience from shopping are stored in habits. You can't anticipate that this will change overnight. It is necessary to develop new habits that fit your new way of life.

The other issue is that, with all the things you're taking into your head every single day, it's filled with things. Let's take a look at clearing the mind and discover what is required to assist you get out of the terrible rut which you're stuck in. It is a fact that there are numerous suffering from depression the present day that medical science is having a hard time staying on top of it. You cannot just take pills and hope all depression will disappear. It's not working that well and for a lot of people who have turned to their doctor for help they're finding doctors now prescribing mindfulness techniques to help patients to overcome depression, instead of prescribing pills to cover up the symptoms of depression. Let's take a look at the responsibilities that your mind is exposed to each day, and then try to cut down on some things that harm your mind:

Advertising

Television

Loud music

Crowd noise

Offices are noisy

Factory noise

Car noise

Your brain is supposed to take everything in, and you could be overwhelmed with information. Add to this the local and political worries that you might have regarding environmental issues as well as all the talk about what you should do to recycle , and you've got the recipe for catastrophe. On top of everything else there is the pressure to keep the pace of everyone else, while all you must be is you. The society has conditioned us to think that we think we need to have the most luxurious automobile, the finest interiors for our homes, the latest technology and even the latest iPhone. We must get away from the pressures. It may sound appealing to you, but it's not real. What if I told you there was a way to attain the same peace in your own home? You'd probably shrug at me and take it for the ride to prove me incorrect. But if you adhere to the guidelines in this book, you'll be amazed that I'm not. The less you have, the better.

Step One: Cleanse the Mind

The method I employ for this is extremely effective and is linked to mindfulness. If the MRI scan was conducted to the brains of Buddhist monks, scientists discovered that they were more content and balanced, and this is because they do not indulge in the same activities that we do, and also because they do mindfulness. In actual fact The Dalai Lama worked with scientists to help them come with solutions to the discontent of the current generation of people. Mindfulness has been proven to be effective , and it's not as complicated or difficult as you think initially.

To let go of all negativity and busy thoughts from the morning until night You must be able to enter the present moment and fully immerse yourself within your own life. This means that if you think regarding the past you have to be able to move away from them . Worries regarding the future play no place in your life. What can you do to achieve this? Simply take a step forward. Let's test to do it the very first time. Relax in a comfortable place. You must align your back to ensure that the energy can flow throughout your body in a correct manner. Then, breathe in through your nostrils until the number 7 and out until you reach 10. It is possible that these numbers are to be a bit high initially however, this type diaphragm breathing can help relax you and, if you can do it for 15 and 20 minutes per day, it will help to unwind your mind. What is the first thing you think about when you breath? The purpose is to focus on your breath, or to step into the present moment. This means that you can focus on your breathing is all you need to do, or focus on what you see from where you're in your seat. Be aware of everything using all your senses. Pay attention to the smell and the environment and the sounds you hear, and the things you feel and see.

We've lost the ability to utilize our senses and we do little to stimulate them.

If this is the first time you attempt this, it may not be very effective as you're not used to it. Thoughts are likely to creep into your head. It is important to let these thoughts drift off. Don't be angry when you can't stop thinking about something. Instead, consider it as an intrusion and then forget about it and go back to breathing in the manner I suggested. It is best to do this after you've eaten, and is best done in the same manner each day.

This helps to boost your energy levels. A less cluttered mind gives you the space to live your the world instead of being overwhelmed by thoughts all the time. If you have any items to be remembered in the course of your day, simply record your thoughts down and let the list provide you with the information that you require at the time you require it. So you don't have to carry around all the extra baggage throughout your day. If you do make a mistake and make amends, after the lesson has been learned then you do not need to be a slave to the error to this day. Clear your mind of any unnecessary clutter.

If you have negative feelings towards someone, now is the right time to let them go. Let them go for what they do. This may seem different from what you're familiar with, but every day, when you encounter situations that increase your anger, you're trying to hold it on and making the person who made you angry control you. When you are able to forgive your anger, the power is gone, and you are larger than the issue and more than just a little more compassionate.

Be aware that what's happened is gone, and what has been yet to happen isn't an aspect of who you are at this point in time. If you're a victim of anger go through them to get to the other side. these negative emotions can be detrimental to your life.

You should be more powerful than them. If you are worried about finances, speak to your partner or find an arrangement that benefits everyone. If you don't have money to pay what you want, but you could make arrangements to pay a little amount per week that will satisfy all. This way you won't feel all these negative emotions in your head. They are released by handling them.

It will be apparent that as you clear your space and simplify your life, it will become easier. The tiny amount of time every day to mindfulness can benefit you in many other ways. If you are feeling negative emotions throughout the day, you are able to return to the state of mindfulness and let those negative thoughts go. Let go can be difficult but you must get back in the present moment. Be aware that each second goes by and that as time passes there are always solutions and you'll not stress too much over the little things. I have heard two women engaged in a fierce argument over the cost in nail polish. This actually broke their relationship and when you think about all of the small factors that lead to the loss of friendships they are nothing when you compare them to the importance of friendship itself. The next chapter guides to reduce the number of friendships so that you can get the most you can from the relationships you do have. You'll be amazed at the way that small adjustments to your personal approach can lead you lead a happier and more satisfying life.

Chapter 10: Learning How to Turn Off

If you've had the pleasure of sitting in a dining establishment and watched people around, you'll realize that a lot often, they do not talk to each other often nowadays. They believe they're doing so, however, what they're actually doing is tapping on the emotions of their iPhones completely unaffected to what's happening in the world that surrounds them. Technology has not only captivated our attention, it has pushed us to a point where we're unable to let it go and just be.

If you're reducing in your daily life and you are feeling down, it is essential to take a walk and appreciate the outdoors more. There's something unique when you go for a walk in the woods, or walking along a river that flows and returning to nature can help you deal with all the issues in a beautiful way. However, many people carry their mobile phones, their laptops, iPads, or computer and are constantly inundated with information overflow. Turn off your device when it's time to turn off. These are the occasions when you must reduce the amount of contact you're in with the outside world, which includes radio, television cellphones, tablets or tablets, as well as computers:

If you're with friends to eat with, you are in a good place.

If you go to visit your relatives

In an interaction

If you visit the park,

If you're in the countryside

If you're at the beach

The issue is that human beings have no way of turning off their devices and must have an amount of silence, or at least a normal conversations throughout their lives. One of my friends had visited her mother in the hospital. Throughout the time the visit was over, she would sneak outside to check her Facebook status updates. While she was joking with her pals she missed an important chance to say goodbye to her mother, who passed away in her absence. We're so busy with all the intrusions of people into our daily lives, that relationships have become less productive ones.

A lot of the emotional stressors that people face today are the result of regret. It's much better to switch off the television when someone in your family needs to speak. It's much better to turn off the telephone if you have a task you need to complete. It's best not to keep an account on Facebook account rather than giving the online friends priority over actual people.

Once you have cleared out all the clutter in your daily life, you have opportunities to take part in activities you might not otherwise undertake. You meet with your friends. You meet people, and become more productive as part of your family as well as your community since you can see beyond the smokescreen and what this world can offer you in terms of entertainment.

If you work at home, set yourself certain time slots so that you can have a life outside of work and in reality doing this you are more productive during your working hours as you split your time and recognize that time spent at the computer is time for work. After your working hours are over and you are free to enjoy the opportunity to unwind from your work and enjoy enjoying more productivity with your loved ones and family.

If you observe a child ignoring you due to being engaged in an online game, think about whether this is the kind of environment you would like to reside in. When you next notice someone not paying attention to a person who is present because they're playing on their tablet or answering calls take a moment to consider whether you require all of this noise within your own life. It will be not. There is no need for anyone to live a life so full of stress that they don't have room for true friendships and family time. It is not necessary to prioritize an individual voice on the other end when it's not important enough. Therefore, get rid of the gadgets which are designed to keep you from the main reason for living. When you do this you will find that you're connected to the world around you and you no longer need to call people or follow them on Facebook because they'll always be around regardless of any gadgets.

Consider what is important to you , and only keep the things you believe to be true. All else is useless. The time you spend watching the TV's screen is time taken from your daily routine. Yes, you can keep the TV but be selective about what you watch , and ensure that your time spent watching is worth your time. There's a lot more you can get accomplished and aren't avoiding doing what you've been meaning to do after you have gotten away from the hold that technology exerts on your life. When I started living a minimalist life I'd say my life has changed. I'm more productive due to the fact that I am more focused. I don't achieve an unforeseen success I focus my efforts around a simple approach which makes success a much easier goal to attain.

Chapter 11: Decluttering Your Home

The more possessions you own the more complicated your life will become. There will be a house filled with items that you don't use anymore or purchased thinking that they fulfilled some function. Then, you realize that you do not really have any use for the things. Have you ever put items away in a drawer, hoping that they'll become use in the near future? What about the objects around you as you relax in a space in your home? Take a look and I'll assure you that your life will not be minimal. In the space where Katy was sitting when she began the process, she could see several things that were preventing her from enjoying the simple things of her daily life. For instance, she owned several different items of collectibles that she had no longer considered the value of each one of them. She began to collect and the bug for collecting was growing. When she first approached me for help she was collecting clocks, match boxes plates and boxes, as well as old toys comics, memorabilia and comics in addition she had everything were introduced to her world which she did not like.

We then looked into her bed. The bedroom was so overcrowded that the room was suffused with the smell of a musty odor, possibly the reason why she didn't sleep effectively. There was clothing that she had worn in her youth, clothes she hoped would be able to fit her in the future, and a lot of furniture. In addition, she had an assortment of designs that muddled the space and made it the worst spot one could ever sit down and relax. The bed linens contrasted with the drapes. The carpets required ripping due to the fact that they were filled with dust caused by an inefficient vacuum cleaner and the rugs which were placed on top of the carpet were completely unsuitable for the area due to their clash with the wallpaper. Katy was exhausted, and it was no wonder. The entire house was suffused with confusion.

De-cluttering the home

If you think there isn't any clutter in your home, take this test. Make three large bin bags or boxes , and go through one room in your home. Determine what items you want to placed in each bag or box in the following order:

Give away things

Things to offer at an estate sale

Things to throw into the garbage

There are numerous charitable organizations that are willing to accept what you see as unnecessary to your daily life. They could be given to those who are unable to afford the cost of furnishing their homes. Clothing could be donated to those who are homeless, and it's worth giving the clutter away to those who could make the most of it. One way to address the issue is to get everything out of your closet, as an example and evaluate the value of the object. There's actually an

Japanese woman who is an organizer. She works on the idea that if a product does not bring you pleasure then you shouldn't use it. It's not a stretch. Once you've finished the closet, move onto the dresser and on until you've cleaned all the rooms in your home. Look at the furniture. Are you really going to need that many furniture pieces in such a small space? If you try to squeeze lots of stuff in a tiny space it will eventually get to the point where you fall over it. It's like a messy mind. Remove things from your home to eliminate clutter. Reduce the size of your furniture. Apply a layer paint to ensure that there's no contrast and always remember that less is always going always be greater.

Then, take a look at the art that is in the room. There will be objects that are sentimental, but when they do not contribute to the day-to-day design and functionality of the space, put them somewhere you will be able to access them at times without letting your life be overwhelmed by the things. It's refreshing. It is indeed. By the time you've finished the room, you'll immediately notice that the space appears larger and you will be able to relax in a space that's free of unneeded clutter. Kate phoned me following our work in her bedroom to inform me that she had had the best sleep she's had in the last ten years in her new bedroom. She had cleared out her belongings off the window and was able to open the window to let fresh air in the space.

It also makes a space more easy to clean as there is no need to be shifting objects around constantly. If you have any items like makeup, or small items, arrange items together in a tray, so that the only thing you need to do is lift the tray up and clean it up, instead of seeing dust accumulate between the various objects. Make sure you are honest, and If you haven't used something in the past 3 months, the chances are that you will not utilize it. In terms of seasonal clothing is concerned, put clothes in your closets that are appropriate for the time of year and utilize vacuum bags for the remainder. This will save space and makes your closets easy to access. You might even find that dress that you thought you gone missing five years back! The mess in your life can obscure the important. If you are unable to let something go consider why, as it's very important. You must be more determined to let go, because once you do, it feels as if you're getting back to square one and that's a an amazing feeling. A couple I worked with believed that they needed to sell their home because it was too small to meet their requirements. After they had decluttered they had altered their minds and concluded that the house was perfect, the same way it was when they purchased it. The issue was not with the house itself. It was the excessive.

Chapter 12: Tracking Earnings and Your Expenditures

It can be a challenge to budget when you've never tried it before. One way to begin is to determine what you're going to start with. To do this, you must be aware of how much cash you are bringing in and also where it will go and every penny of it. The most effective way to accomplish this is to track your trail of paper, including things such as your statements from your credit cards as well as the bank statement for your debit cards as well as checking accounts, as well as any cash you withdraw out from ATMs.

It's not unusual to hear people say they are spending less on items than they actually spend. Consider food, for instance food out on the go, convenient food and coffee at the office can make a lot more than one would believe. You might go through the drive-through to get an everyday cup of coffee on the way to work, and you calculate that $4 per day multiplied by five days per week will cost you an average of $80 per month. This could be true, however is it possible that you are also adding some occasionally (or every day) tip, any drink you might buy for others, or other additional items, like muffins since you'd been in a hurry and didn't have time to eat breakfast? Based on the number of days are in those months, you've been there longer then the twenty days you planned into.

Start with one month

In the first week of each month Make it a habit to save any receipts that you receive. If they don't contain names of the place or it's unclear the purpose of the receipt

Make sure you write down the items you bought. Make a notepad or take note of any cash-paying items you purchase. When you get to the end of the month make a list of everything you have spent money on. Since statements from your credit and bank accounts aren't available until the close of the month, keep your lists in the drawer until you receive your statement. When you receive your statements Sort them out line-by-line and decide the category in which they belong. There should be the standard budgeting categories like:

either rent or mortgage

utilities

car payment

loans (student, home improvement, etc.)

food

clothing

gas

entertainment

miscellaneous

Costs (especially utilities bills) fluctuate every month, so if you can find the previous bills for every month in the previous year, you'll have an idea of what to anticipate for the coming year. In the event that you do not have these then you can call your utility companies and ask for the monthly average. However, you should keep in mind that the utility bills tend to be higher during summer months to pay for air conditioning and in the winter months for heating.

Once you've finished all of this, you'll discern the direction your money is heading. It is possible that you have estimated that your food expenses are significantly lower than they actually are, or you might have not considered how much you spend on clothes. Understanding where your money is going is essential in tracking it and keeping your spending within the budget. This will give you a clear picture of where you are in order to build an image of where you'd like to be.

If you believe that this month isn't typical of the normal ensure you do it again to gauge the true picture.

Tracking Earnings

If you're like the majority of people are, it's simple to monitor your incoming cash flow when you have a regular 40-hour work schedule. For others, like freelancers, who primarily earn tips or are paid on commissions however, it may be more challenging. To determine an easy and near-perfect method to calculate the amount you earn, calculate your total earnings for the previous year and then divide it by 12. It's not exact but it's an overall estimate of what you earn every month. If you're self-employed, be sure to deduct any earnings you have to pay taxes or to your retirement savings and don't put this amount in your income column. Once you've got a clear understanding of the amount you earn on a monthly basis, it's easier to pinpoint the place that your money is going.

It's also relatively easy to create a document using your computer or utilize a piece or paper to write down the amount of money you're receiving. If you work to earn tips, be sure to keep track of them each day you are working, as cash that's not recorded is likely to be lost in the shuffle of your thoughts.

Then Putting It All Together

If you've got a firm grasp of the money you earn and where it is going, it can be refreshing and eye-opening. You might discover you're making far more money than you think or even see obvious signs of the place your money goes that you didn't know about. If you can reduce spending that isn't necessary You will discover that you have more money available to take on your debts to help remove debt. Although paying off debt may be a long process however, it will eventually get you to being able to live the minimalist lifestyle you desire.

The value of a weekly Total Assessment

If you're new to keeping track of their finances and paying off debts it may seem like it's a burden to keep the track of everything. It doesn't need to be a task that demands your time every day the duration of your life. After keeping track of your income and expenses for at least a month and gaining a more complete overview of your financial situation You can then shift to a weekly complete review.

Begin by taking all receipts you have and sorting them into categories. Check your bank account and use the internet to determine what you billed. It's surprising how many people are able to not remember what or how much they charged a few days prior to. It's not a process which should take a significant amount of effort if they've kept receipts the way you ought to. At first the process, it might take longer because you may be unfamiliar with the process however, every week, it will become fasterand you'll spend much less doing it. One of the main reasons for living a minimalist lifestyle is to have more free time and not create additional tasks to be completed. While it might appear as if you're adding a new task on the To Do List, you will actually save your money and making things more valuable that you have to do due to the reduction of unnecessary expenditure.

When you become more organized in how you handle receipts your processes will become more efficient making it easier to save both time and cash. When you are more aware of the places where your money goes you'll have less of a need to conduct a weekly assessment. Some people could go on for years and still be compelled to conduct it, whereas others might only need to do it for a couple of months, and then feel that they're in line with the direction they want to go. Every person is unique, so the duration someone has to take to complete an annual total assessment each week will differ. Some individuals will be happy doing it and observing how much money is spent however it can be an overwhelming task for others who are able to be able to learn quickly and finish it.

When is the best time to end for a Weekly Review

Even when you're no longer in debt and are living the minimalist lifestyle you'd like to live but you shouldn't stop making an assessment regularly. It's crucial to determine the location of any investments as well as the way your retirement funds are performing and whether you'd like to invest more money into something specifically. Certain people perform this every month particularly if they have shares. Others who are more happy to ride the fluctuations of the stock market could only conduct an in-depth analysis once per year. Whatever you choose be sure that it's working for you. If you attempt it every year and realize that's not enough, consider doing it at least every 6 months. There's no single best formula that works for every person. Personally, I've found that once per month is my ideal minimum and it's easy to incorporate this into my routine of bank reconciliation.

Reviewing Your New Lifestyle

While analyzing the numbers is a crucial aspect of budgeting, there's an additional assessment you could be able to conduct. This is to focus on how your quality changes when you alter your outlook While there aren't any particular questions to address, some believe that keeping a journal or an account of their experiences as you transition to a more minimalist lifestyle could truly be an eye-opener. You can keep track of your perception of what's happening and how your bank accounts shift. Write down what you're doing now in comparison to the past and also how you feel about the changes. The entire point of a minimalist way of life is to make things easier, and to live fully without anxiety and excessive consumption. Are you on the right track to that objective? What other areas do you want to tackle? Are you satisfied in your progress and moving forward? These are only a few things you can think about and then write about. You could be surprised at the speed at which you've changed your habits or how quickly you've achieved your goal of paying off the debt. The best part when you make the transition to a minimalist life style is that there's no deadline and each day you're able to be proud of all the achievements you've made on your journey.

The Need to Know - Understanding Why You Need to Know

We as a nation are overwhelmingly drawn to immediate satisfaction. This has never been more apparent than during the severe depression of the 2008-2009. Many people lost everything they could in the stock market, and were not conserving cash in banks as their parents did. There were massive houses being built across the nation and an astronomical level of debt became common. The notion of needing to beat your peers or neighbors was prevalent everywhere. This was in part due to instant gratification. This is something that has become a part of our minds through the years. Instant gratification is the ability to get what you want whenever the time is right, no matter if you have the cash or not. For many people, this included putting money into credit that they should have kept to be used for. It was a matter of taking out loans to purchase a house with a small amount of money instead of the 20% that older generation were instructed to.

The instant gratification process usually begins when you are a child. If parents allow the child who complains or screams at the shop in order to get something, and try to make the child calm down, they offer the child a small piece of candy, leading to the child experiencing instant pleasure. When I have a temper tantrum, I receive candy or toys. It's something that even children of all ages know and can use in their favor. While it might seem innocent to an adult (who simply wants to leave the shop as quickly and with as little drama as is possible) but it actually creates a negative model for the future. We have many adults who don't realize the joy of saving money or paying to purchase something when they are able to make purchases without credit. This is the perfect illustration of wanting as opposed to. need. The fact that you're looking for an upgrade on your car doesn't necessarily mean that you require it. Making the necessary savings for a brand new car and making payments in cash is much more challenging, yet it can cause a lot less financial issues.

True Necessities

If one is living a minimalist life one must be away from the instant satisfaction. Making purchases, whether big or small, should only be made only when they are essential. If your refrigerator is not full, it should be filled with healthy and healthy food items. This is a must. If your refrigerator is full, filling it up with sweets or soda drinks isn't really a necessity, it's a wish. However, this doesn't mean that the minimalist life means you aren't able to take pleasure in things (even soda pop.)...it requires being aware of the differences.

Life's necessities are made up of a handful of things that are essential: an adequate roof food, clothing, and a roof over your head. An adequate roof does not necessarily mean a five-bedroom 4 bath custom home for the family of three. Food, a second necessity isn't about eating out at a 5-star restaurant every week. It's about nutritious food which range from fruits and nuts to vegetables and meats.

The ability to cook can assist those who want to lead an uncluttered lifestyle, in addition, it can significantly impact your budget in a positive manner. The need for clothing is important however, it shouldn't all be brand names. There are a few more expensive clothing items that are top quality basic items that aren't going out of style So if it's more sense to pay an extra amount today instead of purchasing the same thing every year, you'll be able to save money at the end.

Keep in mind that if you've got the basic necessities that you need, there isn't a need for any more. There are certain things we may enjoy or wish for but when one decides to focus on what is essential, it makes demands more evident and may directly affect the budget. If your budget is in order and in order, it's much easy to reduce debt, which makes life less stress-inducing. The focus on simplifying your life could be about buying only what is important and is essential, while having the best moments in life, like the people you love or hobbies that truly delight people.

Chapter 13: General Minimalist Living Tips

If you've accomplished the steps toward becoming minimalist (in depth, may I add) Here are few tips for minimalists that can simplify your life even more.

Tip #1: Don't be a slave to rules that you have been taught.

Minimalism is about simplifying and that's why you shouldn't need to complicate it. You've probably heard of rules like 'you need to restrict your possessions to 100 items' or "you must wear only 33 items over the course of three months'. These should be completely not thought of. Minimalism is a personal choice and when you adhere to its fundamental principles, it will appear naturally.

Tip #2: Don't be afraid by saying "I don't really care" or even 'no.'

This is a tip that will greatly make your life easier if you abide to it. If you and a person are planning something , and they enjoy it more than you, let them decide (after declaring your preferences) If someone attempts to lure you into an task you're disinterested by, inform them that you don't. The art of saying no or letting others plan things without having to control the entire process will save you a lot of time (and lots of time, too!).

Tip #3: Have similar meals

As with clothes and food, thinking about what you should consume can take up your time, causing you to lose the calm mind you treasure so much. To help to manage, you can simply find simple and similar meals and rotate them through the week. If your love is cooking, then get a frenzied in the kitchen, cook, and try new recipes.

Tip #4: Make Things

One of the things we attempt to achieve by minimalist living is to become less dependent on other people and thingsparticularly in our consumer driven society. Learn to grow your own food, master the art of sew and knit, and master the art of fixing things around the home. It will not only increase your dependence on your own abilities, but it can also help you save a few dollars.

Tip #5 Tip #5: Meditate

Meditation is an excellent method to unwind your mind, so it's recommended to make time each morning to practice meditation. Begin with taking a seat in a quiet space for around 5 minutes, engaging in focused exercises like "imagine a fire" or "growing light" etc. Once you're satisfied with 5 minutes, you can increase the time towards 10 or longer! As long as you don't try to fight it, it will be an absolute pleasure for you.

Tip #6: Be content by being in a space that is your own

If you're constantly around people, it may be difficult to keep connected to you. Being content in solitude is the only way to determine what is important to you in your life.

Keep in mind that minimalism is a personal choice and you're the one who decides what is most suitable for you. As with anything new it will always come with obstacles. Simply follow the steps, follow the guidelines and be aware of what is important.

Chapter 14: The Best Way to Sort Trash Into Specific Types

Not everyone collects newspapers. Some people are prone of collecting things that pose a risk or are difficult to dispose of. You might be one of them. If this is the case this chapter is for you. In this chapter, we will discuss various other unusual items that can be a problem when trying to get rid of these items.

Hazardous Waste

It can be one of the toughest aspects to handle. Different cities, and various jurisdictions within a city have different rules and regulations regarding how to handle this kind of waste. Contact your city council or the information office to find out the specifics of your particular zone. In general, however you must be sure you don't cause harm to environmental health or create harm to the infrastructure of your city. For instance, don't dump harmful chemicals or oil in the drain.

Examples of hazardous waste are lights and batteries, car parts paint, used paint accessories chemicals, fertilizers and insecticide. If you've accumulated one of these objects over the years ensure that you dispose of them safely and with care. Different chemicals and various products have their own procedures on what to do with them. So ensure you have the right information prior to dealing with these types of objects.

Furniture

Another instance of unique waste are furniture pieces. As they're typically big pieceslike tables, sofas, mattresses or chairs, your neighborhood garbage person might not want these items. Be aware that you shouldn't be not putting anything out in front of your home so that you don't fall prey to the temptation. If the furniture you have is able to be reused, again go to the local thrift shop to make a donation and give them a new place to live.

Recycling

As we've seen in the previous chapter, items that are recyclable shouldn't be thrown into the garbage. If you do have an extensive collection and recyclables might be able to earn an incredibly small profit from the clean-up. Some facilities will pay you a nice penny in exchange for recyclables. You might want to look through the phone book to determine whether any of these places are near you, and if it's worth it to visit them. In addition certain companies might collect your possessions from your house for you.

Collector's items

If you own an assortment that you are trying to get rid of as you've realized that it's become a habit and you are unable to stop it, you might be able for sale of the objects and could even earn a profit. eBay was created to facilitate this kind of thing and there are a few collectibles that could provide you with a good economic incentive to dispose of the items. It doesn't matter if it's marbles or baseball cards or collectible comic books The online marketplace is where to find buyers.

Whatever it is you have accumulated through the years, be sure you're protected and responsible in getting rid of it. Respect the laws of your city and refrain from doing things that place you, your city's infrastructure, or environmental environment at risk. If you are able to make money from this endeavor, all potential is yours. Do it!

Chapter 15: The Minimalist Lifestyle: How To Live A Simple Lifestyle

Everyday routine of minimalist living

The concept of minimalism is a way of thinking and decluttering an ongoing endeavor. Both can lead to greater focus, more productive work and less stress however, finding the perfect equilibrium between convenience and easy living requires constant adjustment. Like everything that is designed to enhance your life quality being minimalist requires establishing daily routines. This could include physically altering your living space or implementing different thoughts patterns.

It is said that the Free Dictionary defines a habit as an "recurrent and often subconscious pattern of behavior established through repetition." If you commit your self to a particular behavior for a certain amount of time, you'll be able to begin adopting this habit quickly and be unable to stop.

A beautiful, minimalist home can be accomplished in a single swoop the aid of some serious cleaning, but keeping the minimalist look of your home is a different matter. It's a fact of living. It can accumulate quite quickly and that's why adopting certain habits that are mindful at home, such as the five listed below, is vital to preserve the minimalist style and practicality. No matter if you're a veteran minimalist or are looking to get your feet wet in the minimalist movement, these simple habits will ensure your home is looking great.

The Mindful Habit 1:

Clean Your Dishes as Quickly after You're Completely Done

The Minimalist result A definite fact is that nobody enjoys the task of washing a sink full dishes. When you wash your dishes promptly after you've used them, not only is it more simple to keep a clean and clutter-free kitchen, but it also means that you'll use less dishes at first.

Mindful Habit 2:

Be very strict about what You Allow into your home

The Minimalist Results: Maintaining your home as minimalist isn't just about organizing the items you present in your home. It's equally about removing items that you don't require. Be more conscious of the things you'll say yes to. Your space is valuable. Only take in items you truly cherish and are sure to utilize. Don't let your family members dump their possessions on you. Also, take at least 24 hours to think about your purchase before you click confirm your order for that online purchase. It is also possible to reduce unnecessary clutter by sharing your wish lists with your loved ones for birthdays and other important events or by asking them for things (like tickets to a cool performance) instead of stuff.

Affirmative Habit #3:

Sort through emails and mail as soon when You Receive It

Mail is yet another one of those items that piles up quickly, causing a mess in your appearance. Instead of having to sort through an enormous pile of junk mail and bills in the middle of each month, it's far simpler to tackle it on a daily to daily basis. It's only few minutes. It is a good idea to immediately throw away or recycle papers that you do not need. Also, scan and save any important documents could be required to refer to in the future.

If you receive mail that can't be dealt with within less than two minutes, try to identify the task that you have to do to sort it all out and add it to your list of tasks. When it is less than two minutes, then take it off the list, so that it doesn't pile up in your head.

The Mindful Habit 4:

Remove Counter Tops from Counters Each Evening

The Minimalist result It doesn't regardless of how neatly lined-up your appliances in your kitchen counter or how neatly your cosmetics are placed on the toilet sinks, if you have too much stuff that are on your counters, your home can appear very messy. It's a good idea to put things away in cabinets and drawers when not making use of the cabinets or drawers.

5. Mindful Habit #4:

Clear Little Spaces on a regular basis

The Minimalist result: While performing an extensive clean-up of your house in one step is ideal but finding the time for it isn't easy. Don't allow that to stop you from pursuing minimalist living. If you can de-clutter a small area in your house at a time you can still enjoy minimalism happiness. Set aside every Sunday (or every other day during your week) your day to de-clutter and take on one trash storage drawer or kitchen cupboard or shelf in your closet. It doesn't need to be any time in any way. You'll be amazed at the things you can accomplish in just a 15-minute time period.

The art of Minimalism in Everyday Life

If you begin to think of minimalism as a method to be able to focus on what's important to you and not on the notion of letting go of the things you own, everything becomes much more logical. By removing all the things that hinder your ability to achieve your goals and dreams It is easy to live your most fulfilling life, to be your most authentic self , and treat things and people that really value your attention with the care and respect they deserve.

Once we have this settled Let's take a examine some suggestions to go minimal and stay there with positive, meaningful ways.

Minimalist Wardrobe

It's okay if you be a bit embarrassed picking up every piece of clothing and deciding whether it brings you joy, but you should forget about joy for a moment. There are a variety of options to choose which items to keep and which ones to give away. My personal most loved is this classic If I haven't been wearing it for more than an entire year, it is donated to charity.

The way you feel comfortable could be different. Select the outfits that feel amazing and are the most comfortable and will make you feel comfortable and cozy and at home. Eliminate the clothes you only wear when you're running out of clean clothes. But, once you've got there and simplifying your wardrobe will yield a variety of advantages:

It saves the time (and stress!) selecting your outfits to wear for your day.

You'll have less laundry to fold, wash and sort. This saves time and money.

Storage space is freed up to store other items or get rid of the clutter.

You'll always have clothes that make you feel amazing.

After you've streamlined the clothes you wear, these tips will prevent accumulation from getting back.

One in One in, one out. If you purchase a brand new clothing item, place one of your purchases in your charity basket.

Put on your clothes at night to help ease decision stress early in the day.

If you own a washer and dryer, put the clothes directly into the tub after you are done and then load it up after it's filled.

Minimalist Cooking

Put away your pans and pots? Not exactly. According to Taste magazine explains, minimalist food isn't only about simplicity: "the simplicity of the food is in contrast to the effort and thought involved in the preparation." As with all things else, moving towards minimalist kitchens requires making conscious decisions about your beliefs as well as your preferences and time. As with everything else, it is different for different individuals. The most important thing is to think about everything that feeds your family or your own Then decide what aspects matter to you.

It's all about the amount of time you spend in the store. To maximize the amount of time you spend at the store it is best to make an agenda of what you want to buy. What better way to go than and prepare a list of your shopping needs for three days of food. What's the point? Consider a week's worth of food.

Minimalists who plan their meals can also save many money by not buying unnecessary things on impulse and making use of every meal they purchased (without discarding the food waste).

The impact can also be felt on your health. When you plan your meals, be sure to think about what's best for your family and you. A majority of unhealthy foods are bought on impulse, and at a good price in the shops. If you have a plan at hand, you can stay clear of this.

It can take some effort to start simplifying your life however once you begin simplifying, it's much simpler to keep it going. Every step you make will get you one step closer to achieving your goals and living the most satisfying, best life.

Chapter 16: Making Over Bathrooms

A few decades ago, newly built homes typically had one bathroom as well as four or three bedrooms. It has become increasingly commonplace to find every bathroom the number of people living in the house. They can be anything from small closets that are just big enough to fit a toilet and sink or even rooms that are as big as in the main bedroom. Bathrooms with luxury features could have separate shower and bathtub or two sinks that have separate vanities or a massive joint countertop, as well as a separate bathroom with a toilet as well as an access point to your master bedroom closet.

Whatever the size or features the majority of bathrooms in the common American home would benefit from a simple overhaul. Apart from bathrooms that are reserved for guests, the majority of bathrooms have a lot of bathroom amenities and sometimes too much decor for a small area. The purpose of a minimal makeover in bathrooms is creating a peaceful space where you will find a bit of tranquility and peace, even if you just visit for a few minutes.

Step One - Reexamining the subject of towels.

We've previously discussed towels in the process of reorganizing the linen closet, however here , it might be useful to stress that you should not have at least two towels for each household member. One exception could be half bathrooms with only one toilet and a sink. In these cases it is possible to have an additional hand towel or two in the cabinet under the sink. There is probably only one bathmat or rug for each bathtub or shower however, you could store one extra bathmat when absolutely required. Remember that you're working on changing your attitude and to stop storing things "just in the event" you'll need them one day. The likelihood of having these "just in scenario" scenarios ever happening are generally very slim. Keep in mind that you are able to get extra items from family members and family members should you require they. The benefits in reducing the amount of bathmats and towels that you keep in your home will mean less work for you and less anxiety and confusion when you walk into a crowded linen cabinet or bathroom vanity drawer.

Step Two - Reduce your toiletries

Many of us, and especially women have an excessive amount of lotions, hair products as well as products for makeup, body washes including perfumes, hair products, and other personal items for maintenance. Sometimes, we discontinue using a certain product due to the fact that we switch hairstyles, discover about the benefits of a product or even change our preferences. But, we remain loyal to the same product due to numerous reasons we don't know about, many of which we might not be able to determine. Eliminating toiletries that are no longer used can be beneficial not just in the sense of having the bathroom being less messy however, it can also be healthier since older beauty products provide the perfect environment for the growth and spread of bacteria that cause harm. Take these steps to identify which products to keepand which to throw away and which might be able to offer to someone else in a safe manner:

Get rid of old makeup products. One good general rule is to throw away any makeup item that is more than six months. Even if you're making use of it It is likely to have an abundance of harmful bacteria. It's better to think about replacing it with a fresh product as long as your budget permits you to do this. You don't want to compromise the health of your skin and eyes using old, septic products on these delicate areas. Beware of the temptation to share or give away makeup products in the event that they're unopened.

Think about donating or giving some of your used hair products. It may sound to be a bizarre idea however, perhaps you've changed your hairstyle and used only half the expensive hairsprays you bought for your earlier hairstyle. Instead of let the spray get outdated and inaccessible within your bathroom cabinet check whether any of your acquaintances are interested in making use of the product. If they're budget-conscious and are willing to pay for it, they will surely be willing to accept your complimentary hair care products! Another option is to donate to a shelter for homeless people or a non-profit organisation that provides accommodation for families with children admitted to hospitals. These types of shelters may accept used or partially used product for your hair but it's not hurt to inquire.

Reduce the amount of open cosmetics or lotions. Women love to receive fancy-smelling products for their bodies and lotions in the event that they don't know what else to buy to them on their birthdays or at Christmas. This could lead to lots of products that are not opened, and you might or may not use at all. There are many options to think about for such items, as opposed to leaving them in your bathroom or possibly extend their expiration dates. Donate them to the charities mentioned above or to food pantries which distribute food items and household products. These items are also great gifts for those who are trying to find the perfect present for someone you don't know well. Make sure that you don't forget to gift it back for the individual who gifted it to you first!

Get rid of those absurd hotel toiletries. A lot of us like bringing home cute tiny bottles of lotion and shampoo from hotels, particularly high-end establishments. We're thinking about keeping the bottles for guests or trips to the future however, they tend to are tossed aside and seldom used since we'd rather travel with our own personal toiletries. While they're adorable they are, it's the right time to dispose of these tiny bottles. They can be donated easily to a variety of pantries and non-profits.

Stop purchasing in bulk. While it might be economical to purchase hundreds of rolls of toothpaste or toilet rolls in one go but finding the appropriate storage for these items can be a hassle. Instead of being stressed in the search for a place for storing huge amounts of bathing products, you can try to make use of what you have before you purchase a small amount at each time. There may be some extra dollars however the cost is probably negligible if are diligent in your search for bargains. One exception to this principle could be to have a family of 10 If that's the case you'll probably require plenty in toilet paper!

Be sure to dispose of old medicines. Not only do the old medicines create unnecessary space in your bathroom and can be danger to children and anyone else who might be exposed to a mix of medications. For more information on where to dispose of and how to dispose of your old medication visit your local pharmacy, or go to www.fda.org.

Step Three Step Three Minimalist Bathroom Decor

The final touches to your bathroom renovation that is minimalist will require only a few ornaments. No matter how big the bathroom, a little is a lot when it comes to decorating your bathroom. It's easy to get caught up by the plethora of colors or with too many cutesy accessories. It can cause a sense of overwhelm and can be a distraction from tranquility.

Remove all current decorations. Remove any photos or other objects that are hanging on the walls. Also, take down all other items that you've to decorate. This includes candles, floral arrangements and any other catch-all baskets that you have put on shelves or countertops in the bathroom.

Modify the color of your walls If you need to or want to. Be sure to stick with neutral or muted cool hues in order to adhere to the minimalist style or create a sense of tranquility. If you're looking to create a mood that is different try playing around using different shades. Keep in mind that vibrant or bold hues might be too intense for a bathroom, while the dark tone could create a feeling being close to you. The colors can be altered however, so don't be afraid of trying something new!

Put up a few attractive items on the walls. Even in a bathroom that is large it isn't necessary to hang more than a couple of photographs of moderate size to make your walls appear to be complete. In a bathroom that is small the walls could be completely covered by mirrors, towel racks and cabinets for the bathroom already.

Put in a couple of basic elegant and stylish items to decorate as you wish or need. These items also are dependent on the size that the room. If there's room, think about placing a smaller vase, candle or basket on the counter-top or bathroom shelf. The catch-all baskets are an unforgiving nightmare for minimalists because they can quickly become awash with clutter. Whatever you pick be sure to do so with a clear mind and with the goal of minimalism and less stress. Do not just decorate to make it look more appealing. Anything you decide to keep should be valued essential, useful, or valuable. If not, there's no reason to keep the object on display.

Take a moment to take a step back and take a look at the clean-up in your bathroom! We want you to have a peaceful experience whenever you spend any length of time in the bathroom instead of being feeling overwhelmed by the needless towels, toiletries, as well as the chaos that arises due to the hassle of cleaning the mess.

Chapter 17: Minimizing Your Relationships

"Edit your life often and thoroughly. Your life is Your masterpiece, at the end of the day." -Nathan W. Morris Nathan W. Morris Minimalism can help make your stressed or unhappy relationships more healthy, happy and more important. Minimalism is about having relationships that you truly cherish and having time with the most important and positive people that you can count on in your life.

Let's see how you can make the most of minimalism in this area of your life.

Review the various relationships in your Life

Think about the many relationships you have with all your relatives, family members and friends. Evaluate the importance of each one in your the world. Which one is really important to you, and which is burdensome?

There is a person who is always a drag on you but you are unable to avoid them as the financial support they provide you whenever you need it, ask yourself if you really wish to become friends with him/her. If you avoid buying unnecessary items and begin saving money, you won't have to rely on his/her assistance and won't have to endure all the insults they throw at you.

Additionally, think about all relationships that matter to you, but you've not given enough time to them recently. Do you sacrifice your time with your family? Do you rarely meet with your kids on a regular basis and let them feel unimportant? If so, it's time to shift your priorities and pay attention to the ones who really matter to you.

Gradually distance yourself from people who don't mean your life to you, and who are a source of discouragement in any way. Also, give more attention to all the positive, loving and positive people in your life.

Have a relaxing time without a phone with loved Ones

If you've reviewed your relationships and made the decision to end them and keep some, set aside more time to spend with your loved ones. Make sure that your time spent with them is devoid of gadgets, phones or social media. If you're not watching a film with your family as well as sitting in the same room with your children while you check your smartphone, you should spend genuine, time-based moment with your children.

If you prefer to have a meal with your spouse, listen at what she is saying, and relate your own experiences and tales. If you begin talking and listening with your loved ones, you will get to know them better and begin to appreciate the company of your loved ones too. This can help you gain satisfaction from them , instead of relying on devices and gadgets that do not make you feel happier or relaxed.

Talk with Your Loved Ones regarding Minimalism

When you introduce minimalism into your life, discuss the changes with your family members. Let your family know that you're living a minimalist existence and you'd be thankful if they could follow the same path. Instead of requiring them to adopt this lifestyle start by setting an example by following your own example first. When your children witness yourself being content with less things like clothes, gadgets and other items and they'll be inspired to be the same.

If your family members also are a minimalist, you will be more likely to adhere to it and you will be happy for the rest of your life. To maintain your clutter-free life begin to bring simplicity to your professional as well as your financial life. The next chapter will show you how to achieve that.

Chapter 18: Redefining Your Lifestyle

"You tell yourself, 'If only I could have a bit more, I would be very happy. But you make an error. If you're not satisfied with the amount you have it is unlikely that you'd be content if it was multiplied." -- Charles Spurgeon. 1834.

Making a change to your Financial Situation

Finance is the underlying element of our modern society. We are always in need of it and are always spending it. Life's quality is often determined by how much wealth one is able to accumulate. The problem with having too much could be due to people having be arrogant and self-centered. The accumulation of money may feel like an unending cycle, slipping deeper as you accumulate more possess. Making the switch from a life of excess could transform your life. If you're looking to save money to meet a financial goal, choosing to be healthier is likely bring you a lot of money. There is no need to change the way you live your lifestyle. There are a few things that you must master to reduce. A commitment to your goal and overcoming anxiety about what's not common, and setting goals to inspire you to continue and observing the guidelines you have set for yourself.

Exercise is an excellent method to cut back. It doesn't necessarily mean signing up for an expensive gym and increasing your expenses. Do not pay for gym memberships when exercising can be done anywhere and involves basic actions. Instead of spending money on fuel when you drive to run and do your shopping, take a walk or run to burn off calories. Take part in games and outdoor activities in your local communities to gain fitness while also saving money.

Take a look at your daily routine and find out the expensive and ineffective habits you're engaging in. If you are spending money every day on unhealthy food items, soft drinks or smoking cigarettes Reduce your consumption and find you have money to save. Cut down on your drinking habits or completely cut off your drinking. Avoid sales as they make you believe that you're saving money however you'll end up spending more money in the end.

Reduce the frequency you visit restaurants for a meal or take a delivery. Introduce cooking at home to your menu plan. Shopping for groceries and cooking yourself meals can be more affordable than purchasing ready-to-eat meals and transportation costs. This also helps reduce calories as the majority of people prefer ordering fast food. Your budget for meals can be reduced by half if you begin making yourself meals.

Make the switch to fresh foods. Food processed typically adds to the amount of calories consumed and also the excess amounts of salt, fat and sugar. There is a misconception that eating organically is more expensive than other options. The main thing to remember is the decision. Avoid organic food items sold in shops or at supermarkets. Explore local markets and choose the items you want at an affordable cost. Choose products that are in season. This is especially true for fruit. In the event that you do not, you could pay a lot more for non-seasonal fruit and vegetables.

If your workplace offers health benefits for employees make the most of the chance to save money on health insurance. This is applicable to retirement benefits too. There are other methods of saving within an organization by way of financial programs, where employees are advised to save a small amount out of their earnings towards more health insurance and can be used to supplement retirement savings following their retirement.

Make every effort you can to free yourself of your debt. The burden of debt makes it hard to save up money for vital things. The majority of people are born carrying the burden of student loans upon their backs. After cutting unnecessary expenditure and saving enough money to save for the rainy days and then start repaying the debts who owe you and any other debts that you've accrued over time. It is not necessary to repay everything in one go however, paying off your debts must be a top priority.

Don't use credit cards in lieu of cash. It might be a safer alternative, but credit card companies constantly tempt you into spending more than you actually need to and are followed with hefty interest and charges. Credit cards are a better alternative, or you can keep cash. Only spend the amount you have to because you are only spending what you have.

Automatize your finances, and you're less stressed spending time thinking about financial matters. Begin with small steps to automate the process of making deposits and bill payments. Work on it until you've got a largely paper-free system. This eliminates the mess that you've accumulated and provides a safer system for managing finances. You can track your transactions online, and you won't need to be concerned about the loss of receipts. Make sure you check your accounts regularly to make sure that everything is working smoothly.

Always keep a budget in mind when you go shopping. If you're trying to improve your financial resources, make sure you don't overspend more than what you make. Budgets apply to all, not just those with six figures. Do not get caught in the trap of consumption. Only purchase what you really need, but only if it's affordable for you.

Remember that it's not necessary to complete all of these tasks at once. Be patient when implementing the change to ensure that you are able to adjust to it. These changes are designed to last a long time and there isn't any need to rush.

You don't need to have multiple bank accounts. Pick four accounts in case you require several accounts. Monitoring the financial activity of many banks can be a challenge. Make sure you only have the information you require and keep an eye on it.

Do not let money take over your life. True happiness and pleasure can't be purchased. Making it the single most important thing over all other relationships is not the right approach to live your life. Find a job which is satisfying to you instead of the high salary. Choose to focus on your passion rather than about success. Budgeting and reducing your spending will make your life easier, and you'll find that you can live a easier and healthier lifestyle.

Minimalism Means Freedom

A simple lifestyle does not mean removing all enjoyment from your life. It is simply about putting greater value on things that have significance. When we determine the most important things in life you can enjoy freedom that others seek but will never find. Freedom from stress and be more imaginative, no distractions, and freedom from negative thoughts or any other kind of freedom you desire and can attain by being minimalist.

Opportunities to pursue your passions and interests are created by the letting go of unnecessary things that take up your time. It is inevitable to grow when it is the time to focus on the things that bring value and satisfaction. It is possible to look within ourselves to discover who we are as well as what we are.

Spending time with friends and family members we love allows relationships to grow and become stronger. We are more aware and aware of what is going in the world in the world around us. It is easier to be able to appreciate the world and our lives when we are able to see the things that happen.

Peace is found through the freedom that comes from living in a minimalist way. There are no chains that hold us to one spot or an enumeration. We are free to pursue whatever we like to achieve our goals. We are free to travel, investigate as well as change and become better individuals. Freedom of mind and finances allow us to live on little , and to make the changes we require. No more in the process of earning money at a job which we do not like. It's about making our self and those in our lives satisfied. We do more for others while we do less.

The discovery of our own self allows us to start our journey towards self-satisfaction. Anything we accomplish as minimalists will provide us with some sort of value. We know our reasons to accomplish things.

We're more connected with our community. We share positivity and encourage others to follow our example. We do the best we can to help others and are rewarded with happiness. We are concerned about the earth as it is in its own way the earth cares for us.

A lot of people think that minimalistism is boring. It's not. If people just see the superficial aspects of what minimalism means and are prone to make assumptions about the concept. They see the casual way of life, the lack of social interaction as well as the semblance of bland decor, and make false assumptions about it. It's not about what's physically present and what we get when we simplify our lifestyle. There are different kinds of minimalism that a variety of personalities are able to accept.

Making the Change

Now, you're feeling overwhelmed by thoughts of changing your life. You're unhappy with your present life. You're looking to make changes. But you aren't sure where to begin. You're beginning to feel overwhelmed by the choices and are considering reversing. Do not give up. take the next step to make a change in your life effectively.

Find out the most bizarre aspects of your daily life. Examine areas that you've never visited and begin to look at what's missing or needs to be fixed. Keep a list of the things that may have led your life and establish goals.

What is the reason that inspired you to make the decision to alter your life? Most of the time, there are obstacles that we can't seem to conquer that cause us to look at ourselves in a different way. Be honest when you make these assessments as they can be a catalyst for how to improve.

In this assessment You will realize that some aspects that you live in are more in comparison to other areas. Your social life could be in decline while your work life is going well. You'd like to alter your appearance and be healthier. Be honest about these differences since only you are in control of your life.

Do you have a reason to make the change? Are you looking to master new skills? Do you wish to explore more? A goal helps you determine how you can transform and helps you to reach your desired goal.

It's all about commitment. There are many legitimate reasons to want to change, but without committing you'll never achieve anything. The idea of leaving our comfort zones may be intimidating however it's not difficult. Remember the reward in the close of the journey.

The process of going through it gives an opportunity to discover more about your own personality. You discover how much you are willing to put up with and what your goal in life really is, and how determined you are to see an event happen. It also helps us review our assumptions. These beliefs can propel us forward or push us back. We can be encouraged and weed out the false beliefs that can hinder our growth.

Keep in mind that there will always be obstacles difficult to conquer. It's regular part of life. Do not give up at the first sign of difficulty or be afraid of failing. Make a mental picture of the result you'd like to achieve and hold that vision in your the mind of your. It will guide you through the toughest of times.

There are certain things you should be aware of as you're going through the transformation process.

Your attitude will determine the success or failure of your work. The more positive you radiate and the more positive outcomes you're likely to achieve.

Your emotional intelligence helps to comprehend and manage your own emotions, while knowing the feelings of other people. It is a skill that must be developed over time to reap the rewards. Consider how you respond to your decisions and thoughts, and observe how this affects your happiness.

Remember that often reactions can affect the way you think. To change your life, you'll be required to alter how you respond to events and situations. You can't alter the outcome but you can be able to react to it however you want and thus alter the result completely.

Be aware of when you should let go. It's not the same as surrendering. You don't have to always be successful. If you're struggling with something that's taking your energy away There is no sense in continuing to fight for it.

It is important to express the way you feel. Let your anger, discontent and frustrations to a trusted person and this helps keep things straight and relieves the burden that was in your head for a long time. This will allow you to maintain an optimistic outlook and become more determined to make changes.

Be grateful for everything and everyone you are blessed with. There's always someone that is less fortunate than you.

Positive reinforcement and gratitude can enable you to live an enjoyable and positive life.

How can you be sure you adhere to the plan? Set achievable goals. Do not chew more than you're able to chew. There's only a limit to how much you can take in. Be happy throughout the process. Do not take yourself too seriously and be jolly. Keep your family and friends close by to help you. They should be supportive of your decisions and encourage you to be more effective. Don't allow negative influences to surround you. If you are able get help, consult a coach. It's always a good idea to have someone professional around.

Many of the beliefs we believe about ourselves as well as others have hindered our path through life. We look at progress and achievement in comparison to the achievements and progress of other people. We begin to believe that we're not capable enough to achieve what we want, and stop trying to get these goals. It's time to start altering your perspective. Consider yourself as a person who is free of the notion about "anyone other than you." Trust in yourself and stay true to your story. Utilize your emotions to help you tell your story. But, you won't achieve anything if you just think about it. Put into the work. Make yourself a challenge and be assertive regarding what you would like to achieve. Keep yourself motivated and stay optimistic.

Chapter 19: What to Begin By Living A Minimalist Lifestyle

Many people across the world live a life that's not even as good as the one presented in the text. There's a high possibility that each inch of empty space is covered in various clutters and those who reside in homes like this have a list of other things they'd like and they'll be hesitant about spending their hard-earned money on. There's no reason not to want high quality of life, however it must be earned.

If you've read to this point, you know the reason why hoarding can be a problem, and why it doesn't always make someone happy. It is best to begin at the earliest possible point to make the changes that are needed to your life. Here are the steps for clearing out the clutter and begin the path of living a minimalist lifestyle.

Declutter!

The term "clutter" has been mentioned numerous times throughout the book however it's necessary to use it in order to emphasize how big of an issue it's. It's fine to have nice things but it's important to be aware of what is important and what's not.

It's easy to carry out an experiment. Go to any room within your home now and smooth any surface you can reach with your hands. It could be any type of surface and it doesn't matter whether it's a desk or chair. Check out the things placed on the surface, and then decide to eliminate all of them. It might feel strange and uncomfortable at first , and you'll likely come up with reasons the need for each of these items even though you haven't utilized them for years. It is nevertheless essential to get rid of the majority of them to continue your experiment.

After you have removed the things you decide to take away, you'll be able to see that the area is much more appealing, and not just a bit better. The space you create is for those things you really are passionate about, and they stand out as they are worthy to to be so. There's a high chance that you couldn't be able to see the surface before , and you're able to be able to see it now as you've cleared away lots of clutter. it is much easier to look at and also on the mind , and can make you feel a lot more comfortable.

The things you choose to keep are the ones that you value and are your most valuable part of your home. This way your average worth of the items and belongings on the surface will increase. These items are now likely to have the chance of being utilized more as they'll look like they are important instead of disappearing into the clutter.

Also, it is the fact that cleaning will be easier to handle since the time comes to clean away dust from the surface you'll only need to take off a few things and need to replace only some items once you're done. The time needed for cleaning is reduced by half, and you can focus on items that are important. Imagine what could be accomplished with this method for your entire home. To take this exercise further, you can do the same for each surface in the area of your preference.

Eliminate the Boxes

There's a reason clearing clutter can be beneficial and this is the best way to gain your mind clear. Our brains are wired to look for something to be attentive to and then filter out items that merit being attentive to from things that don't merit being given attention. If it's not easy to discern what's important and what's not so, the brain releases higher levels of stress hormones. The more noise and clutter it is there, the more the brain is required to process all the information. This could lead to burnout especially when a person is exhausted after a long day, and all one would like to do is unwind.

A lot of clutter is a lot of work, and that's why it's not always better in the quantity of things that we have in our lives and homes. There are plenty of objects that seem innocent but can cause stress, even though you do not know it. An example is numerous boxes you have around your house. You may think that boxes are a good option to have because they make storage easy and allow you to take more items out of your space. However, the reality is that boxes may make more clutter and make it difficult to work.

The boxes will collect lots of dust if they do not have lids on. More important is that they are objects and things that aren't essential are likely to be a nuisance and take up your thoughts. It is possible to conduct an experiment by finding each box and then moving them away from your thoughts. Once you've done this then take a moment to observe how tidy and peaceful your house has become. It is important to search the rooms for boxes, as there's the possibility that they are in areas where it's easy to overlook the boxes, like under the bed and on the tops of shelves.

This is easy, however, the outcomes are more complicated. One of the benefits from getting rid of these boxes is that cleaning in the future will be much simpler and will be much quicker. It is important to determine the factors that create stress and increases the amount of noise, even if you don't see it clutter.

Control Your Cables

Cables are something that even minimalists can get very annoyed by and it's crucial to control those cables in some manner so that you don't end up with cables that cause horror. There's a high possibility that you have cables around your house that you've completely put away when it comes to organization related.

But, these cables create an eye-strain and make your home appear less neat and organized if they're not managed in a proper manner. There are ways to handle those tangled cables. Boxes are a great option to store the cables. You can also connect those cables to the back of the desk and connect cables to backs of equipment like monitors. A suitable solution to cables is different for every person. Hence it is important to be creative to maximize space.

One In One Out Rule

If you're looking to ensure that your house is clean, you'll need to set up certain guidelines and adhere to these rules. "One in, one away" rule is one of the rules that you must definitely adhere to you to reach your aim of having a clean home. The rule is easy to follow and involves taking one item off for every new thing you purchase. This will help you maintain the quantity of items in your home under control to avoid becoming a into the trap of burnout.

In doing this, you'll also save money if take the initiative to sell the thing you're removing. So, you won't have to think about creating space to store a new product since each when you purchase the latest item there is a space that must be created. This can force you to contemplate what is essential to you and are worthy of keeping.

This might appear to be a bit extreme however, you can test it and when you've seen the results you'll have no doubt in your mind as to this being the correct way to go.

Eliminating Things

If you follow these steps and you'll see that you're eliminating a shocking amount of stuff. It is imperative to point out the fact that this process isn't simple. It isn't easy for the majority of people.

To begin the process, you need to start with a bang. You must conduct a massive cleaning up that allows you to can quickly eliminate lots of things. This is a great way to set the stage for your home and life and gives you a new start. It is extremely effective because people enjoy the feeling of a fresh start and the possibility of a new adventure.

The first step to clearing out is filling the storage containers with things that have sat in box for far too long, and is likely to not be ever for a while. If an item hasn't been used for more than 6 months and is not being used, it must be placed into the storage box. Items that have sentimental value or have a high value in terms of money are an exception to this policy however.

The key to getting rid of objects is to take it easy because you might hesitate and then take a long time to are unable to contemplate all day. Before throwing away the items the items, consider what objects are able to be sold at an acceptable price. And If they could, you must keep them in order to make it possible to sell them as quickly as you can. Anything left over is able to be donated to an organization or recycled to be used for good.

When selling your products do not try to sell every item because looking through every item and assessing it could cause additional stress and increase the chance of ending the entire process.

Conclusion

The book you purchased will help you make your life easier, save money, travel more and feel more confident. If you're not downsizing at the moment, DO it now! The best time to get started is right now. Are you able to think of compelling reasons not to? If you keep putting the task off, it's going to become more difficult to gain the momentum you have now. If you choose to do this you'll be part of the extremely elite class of "doers" rather than the "talkers" class that the majority of people are a part of. You will be able to escape the costly consumerism that has the majority of Americans stuck in debt. If you're struggling with debt (like the majority of us) it is an effective option to begin the path of reducing and getting rid of debt. Once you've reduced the size of your belongings, you could choose to reduce the size of your home. The result is a smaller rental or mortgage payment, and you'll pay less on utility bills and maintenance of your home. In the end, you are in charge of your future and not the possessions that you have. Consider the new lifestyle that you will be able to live with no burden of clutter you've accumulated. All you have to do is act. Once you've got going, I am certain you'll find it simpler than you imagined. It's not because it's simple, but because you're a strong person with the determination to achieve it. We tend to avoid situations like this, but once you've done it you will find it simple. The process of downsizing is 80percent mental and 20 percent physical. Once you've conquered the mental aspect, you'll be able to accomplish various other activities. Best of luck with your new, less-cluttered life!

www.ingramcontent.com/pod-product-compliance
Lightning Source LLC
Chambersburg PA
CBHW071841080526
44589CB00012B/1080